What Would Rob Do?

An Irreverent Guide to Surviving Life's Daily Indignities

ROB SACHS

WILEY

John Wiley & Sons, Inc.

Published by John Wiley & Sons, Inc., Hoboken, New Jersey
Published simultaneously in Canada

Illustrations © Joshua C. Otto.

For general information about our other products and services, please contact our Customer Care Department within the United States at (800) 762-2974, outside the United States at (317) 572-3993 or fax (317) 572-4002.

Wiley also publishes its books in a variety of electronic formats. Some content that appears in print may not be available in electronic books. For more information about Wiley products, visit our web site at www.wiley.com.

Library of Congress Cataloging-in-Publication Data:

Sachs, Rob, date.
   What would Rob do?: an irreverent guide to surviving life's daily indignities / Rob Sachs.
      p. cm.
   Includes index.
   ISBN 978-0-470-45773-3 (pbk.)
1. Conduct of life—Humor.   I. Title.
   PN6231.C6142S24 2010
   814'.6—dc22

                                                          2009028780

Printed in the United States of America

10 9 8 7 6 5 4 3 2 1

For Anna

CONTENTS

Introduction   1

1. Wrong Place, Wrong Time   8

Stains on Your Shirt! What Would Rob Do?   10

Stepped in Dog Poop? What Would Rob Do?   14

Stuck in an Elevator? What Would Rob Do?   18

Speeding Tickets: What Would Rob Do?   21

Stuck in the Middle Seat of an Airplane? What Would
   Rob Do?   25

2. Wooing Woes   31

Avoiding a Chick Flick: What Would Rob Do?   34

Making a Great Playlist: What Would Rob Do?   36

Winning Carnival Games: What Would Rob Do? 41

Surviving on the Dance Floor: What Would
   Rob Do? 46

Cooking a Romantic Meal: What Would Rob Do? 49

Matchmaking? What Would Rob Do? 53

Singing a Love Song Like Air Supply: What Would
   Rob Do? 56

3. Dude, Get a Grip! 62

Playing Poker: What Would Rob Do? 64

Eating at a Buffet: What Would Rob Do? 66

Eating Hot Peppers: What Would Rob Do? 69

Coming Up with a Catchphrase: What Would Rob
   Do? 73

Underdressed for a Party? What Would Rob Do? 77

Getting Past the Nightclub Bouncer: What Would
   Rob Do? 80

Ordering a Macho Drink: What Would Rob Do? 83

Playing Pickup Basketball: What Would Rob Do? 86

Naked in Public? What Would Rob Do? 90

Flea Markets: What Would Rob Do? 93

4. You Have Only Yourself to Blame 97

Conquering Bad Habits: What Would Rob Do? 100

Need a Public Restroom? What Would Rob Do? 102

Big Fat Zits: What Would Rob Do? 106

Snoring: What Would Rob Do? 110

Forget Someone's Name? What Would Rob Do?   114

I Clogged the Toilet and I'm at a Party! What Would
Rob Do?   118

Got Clutter? What Would Rob Do?   122

Protecting Your Voice: What Would Rob Do?   128

Getting Fit and Losing Weight: What Would
Rob Do?   130

Passing Gas: What Would Rob Do?   133

Combing the Coif: What Would Rob Do?   137

5. Slipups in the Spotlight   141

Performing Onstage: What Would Rob Do?   145

Karaoke Night: What Would Rob Do?   149

Giving a Wedding Toast: What Would Rob Do?   153

Planning a High School Reunion: What Would
Rob Do?   157

Leaving a Good Voicemail Message: What Would
Rob Do?   160

Talking through Cyberspace: What Would
Rob Do?   165

It's *Ponch*! Meeting a Celebrity: What Would Rob Do?   169

American in London? What Would Rob Do?   175

6. Daddy Dilemmas   179

Naming Your Baby? What Would Rob Do?   181

My Wife Is in Labor! What Would Rob Do?   186

Buying Kids' Clothes: What Would Rob Do?   191

Annoying Kids' Music: What Would Rob Do?   193

Having a Life While Being a Dad: What
Would Rob Do?   198

Epilogue: What Would Rob Do . . . Next?   203

Acknowledgments   206
Index   209

Introduction

Long before I ever thought of writing a book about life's daily indignities, I had the idea to talk about them on the radio—well, more like the Internet. I've been hosting *What Would Rob Do?* podcast for National Public Radio since the spring of 2005. Each episode explores the unfortunate circumstances we encounter every day such as forgetting someone's name, figuring out what to do when you get a zit, or trying to write a good wedding speech.

You may be wondering how I became a correspondent of conundrums. I certainly didn't set out to follow these types of stories. After graduating from college, I took a job at NPR and moved to Washington, D.C. I had this grand vision that in no time I'd be hosting my own radio show, making guest appearances, handing out tote bags, leaving my voice on other people's answering machines . . . in essence, serving as NPR's voice to young America (a demographic they really needed to court). When I arrived, I found myself instead manning the help desk for NPR's satellite network. This job consisted of sitting by the phone and waiting for stations to call and tell me they missed the feed of *Thistle and Shamrock* (the popular Celtic music show) and ask whether they could order another transmission. You have to start somewhere. Through this position I finagled my way onto the programming side of things, working behind the scenes on shows such as *Morning Edition*, *All Things Considered*, and *Talk of the Nation*.

Eventually I moved to Los Angeles, where NPR was opening up a new bureau in Culver City. I started as an assistant producer on the launch of a (sadly now defunct) news show, *Day to Day*. On the program, I produced a segment called "The Unger Report" with Brian Unger, formerly a correspondent for *The Daily Show*. My job was to find offbeat stories for us to cover. On one of our first outings we went to a West Hollywood salon that specialized in spray-on tans. Brian felt that to really capture the essence of the story, one of us needed to go through the procedure. He promptly volunteered my services. Only later did I realize that it might have been wise to have been equipped with a Speedo or something to cover my delicates. After a few days my *whole* body had turned a brownish-orange hue.

The piece turned out to be a hit, and soon Brian and I were out looking for stories that involved an element of danger and/ or embarrassment. Over the course of a few months, I straddled a live rodeo bull for a segment on professional bull riding, had my arm twisted around my head for a piece on Krav Maga (Israeli martial arts), and had my hair sizzled with a straightening iron for a segment on men's Hollywood hairstyles. If Ryan Seacrest could do it, so could I, right?

It didn't take long before I realized that I was on to something. My participation in the reports was providing more than just funny sound bites; I was also sharing useful information on what to do and, as was the case in many instances, what *not* to do. I started to think that I had something to offer listeners if they ever found themselves in similar sticky situations. What I lacked was a way to convince NPR that they needed to share my vision with the world.

Then came the memo. Had I known it was going to be such a life-altering, company-wide e-mail, I would have saved it in my in-box, or at least printed it out.

In 2005, NPR decided it was time they put more serious effort into expanding their presence on the Internet: "We're starting up an initiative to do more podcasts, so please submit your proposals if you have an idea." (A podcast is a radio show you can download onto your iPod.) And so *What Would Rob Do?* was born. The podcast began with little fanfare, but it quickly garnered a few hundred listeners. Since then I've been able to grow the audience to around twelve thousand a month, and the numbers continue to rise.

The podcast expanded far beyond my adventures with Brian Unger, and grew to include knowledge from my vast wealth of humiliating life experiences. Over the years I've found innumerable ways to be embarrassed and emasculated, but I also recognize that recounting my pitiful experiences doesn't necessarily bring the listener any closer to potentially conquering my type of predicaments. That's why I bring in a ringer for each episode, an expert in the field to help illuminate where I went wrong.

I've talked to everyone—from the maker of Dave's Insanity Sauce, Dave Hirschkop, about how you should properly eat hot peppers, to Jennifer Wilson, a world-class opera singer, on how to protect your voice. To fulfill my '80s childhood dreams,

I spoke to my own A-list of celebrities, including Erik Estrada from *CHiPs*, who helped set me straight on how to act around a celebrity, as well as Tom Wopat from *The Dukes of Hazzard*, who gave me tips on how to not screw up your lines when acting. I also chatted with Michael Buffer, the "Let's Get Ready to Rumble!" guy, who helped me unlock the secrets to finding a cool catchphrase.

Many times these experts affirmed and validated things I had learned the hard way—like not telling the cop who just pulled me over for speeding that I forgot to look at the speedometer. More often than not, though, the experts offered some great insider tips. For instance, I now know that professional hot pepper eaters coat their mouths with vegetable oil before a competition. And then there was Fabio, who in the course of a conversation about how to not be underdressed for a party offered little in terms of practical advice, but did a lot to confirm my previously held stereotypes about male models.

Now that you're aware of some of the better-known names who will be popping up in the book, I think it's also worthwhile to include an introduction to the people around me who most often shoulder the burden of my naiveté; I speak of my family. Over the years I've been doing the podcast, I've found that some of the best advice I've gotten has been from my own kin, all of whom have their own areas of expertise.

I grew up in a nice Jewish neighborhood outside of Philadelphia with my two older siblings, Andrea and Mike. Like most kid brothers, I grew up idolizing Mike despite the fact that our interests were almost completely opposite. Since high school, Mike has been hooked on cars, fitness, and finding ways to live the VIP lifestyle. I was much more similar in personality to my sister, who was interested in music, books, and movies. In addition, Andrea appointed herself to the role of second mother to me (not surprisingly, she was the first one of us to have kids of her own). Now that I'm a dad too, she and her husband, Josh, give me lots of great parenting advice.

As for my actual mother, she's a native New Yorker and an avid tennis player and has a master's degree in art education. A lifelong teacher, Mom is loving and caring but a tough disciplinarian. When we were growing up, she would make us cower with her signature disapproving look that involved raising one eyebrow and cocking her head to the side as if to say, "Don't you even dare." My dad is more of an easygoing guy. His main interests are golf, traveling, and running the family business. Along with my uncle Keith, he owns a company that sells packaging to the wine and liquor industry, an offshoot of a company started by my grandfather.

My family members still have a lot of influence on me, but these days the person I have by my side for just about every situation is my wife, Anna. She grew up in the Berkshires in western Massachusetts, which gives her small-town sincerity along with an appreciation for arts and culture. She also has a competitive spirit that comes from being a track star in high school. One of the things I appreciate most about Anna is her patience and understanding, both as the mother of our daughter, Rachel, and as the wife of a guy who has a knack for continually finding brand-new ways to embarrass himself.

Now back to the book. It follows up on the topics from the podcasts and expands a lot on things that I didn't have time to fit in my segments. The majority of the podcasts fall into a set of distinct categories, ranging from dealing with personal predicaments like contending with a bad haircut to embarrassing situations such as getting a stain on your shirt or stepping in dog poop. There are also dilemmas that relate to trying to be macho, trying to find romance, or figuring out what to do when you are thrust into the spotlight. I added a new category when Anna gave birth to Rachel. Now there are tons of new-daddy dilemmas that I encounter every day.

It seems that anything can qualify as a daily indignity. While I sometimes stretch the basic meaning of "indignity" to include a number of different scenarios, there are a few guidelines I usually try to follow:

1. It must truly be an indignity without an easy solution. While this sounds simple enough, it's not. A lot of people have given me suggestions for topics like: what would you do if you walked into the ladies' room by accident? I'd simply turn around and walk out. Good candidates for a *What Would Rob Do?* indignity require a more complex scenario where the solution often involves a mixture of know-how and some improvisational techniques.

2. Not successfully solving the indignity must result in further humiliation from the situation you're in. Your pride has to be at stake, like when you get up on stage on karaoke night. You either sink or swim there.

3. Success in overcoming the indignity not only saves you from embarrassment but also gives you some genuine bragging rights (for example, getting past a bouncer at a club, or talking your way out of a speeding ticket).

4. Last, a *What Would Rob Do?* indignity should involve the need to master a new skill set or a really cool talent to make up for your ineptitude, such as becoming the master streetballer at your local basketball court.

Ideally, this book will become your handy survival guide, something you can tuck away in your backpack or briefcase (or fanny pack, if that's your thing). If what you read here helps you avoid some of my missteps the next time you encounter one of life's trickier moments, I've accomplished my goal. If reading about my less-than-proud moments reminds you of something you've done yourself and makes you feel less alone, then I've also succeeded. And even if you already know how to avoid many of these situations, I hope you'll still enjoy reading about them, perhaps finding some amusement in my own unfortunate path to self-enlightenment.

1.

Wrong Place, Wrong Time

Whenever someone asks me what *What Would Rob Do?* is about, I always tell them it's about how to deal with situations that happen to you all the time but that nobody really tells you how to deal with. A lot of these things are not necessarily your fault. Call it bad luck, misfortune, or just the law of averages, but sooner or later a disconcerting circumstance will occur. You can either be caught helpless or have a little bit of knowledge to help you out of the jam.

Take the unfortunate scenario of getting a stain on your shirt. You could be having a completely enjoyable evening out with friends, perhaps eating Chinese food and—bam!—some of General Tso's chicken lands right on your new shirt. I spoke to one of the country's premier dry cleaners to find out how to fix the problem.

And speaking of unexpected messes, have you ever stepped in dog poop? You can take every precaution in the world—always look at the ground, be extra mindful around fire hydrants, never play pickup football in a dog park—yet it's still bound to happen. According to a 2009–2010 survey by the American Pet Products Manufacturers Association, there are 77.5 million pet dogs in the United States; so even if 99 percent of pet owners bag their dog's poop during their twice-a-day walks, that still leaves nearly one and a half million poops unaccounted for each day across the country. That's a whole lot of stink.

Surprising indignities extend far beyond the dog park; they can happen anytime you step outside your house. Anytime you get in the car, you have to worry about what to do if you get pulled over for speeding. You only have a few moments to think through what you'll say as you sit in your car watching in the mirror as a state trooper approaches your driver-side window with notebook in hand. Perhaps you could tell him about a survey done by Purdue University that showed the majority of people believe it is okay to drive at least five miles over the posted speed limit. Then again, it's unlikely that the excuse really will hold up against an officer who feels personally offended by your cavalier approach toward accelerating. But what can you actually say or do to get out of this ticket? With a little help from the California Highway Patrol, I'll offer a few ideas.

It seems there's no escaping problematic scenarios. Even indoors, we're still susceptible to being tripped up. I heard from a musician who found herself stuck in an elevator in San Antonio, of all places. I discuss what you can do if you're in this situation—other than write a country song about it. Lastly in this chapter, I'll take a look at one of the most unpleasant spots to be in: the middle seat of an airplane.

I hope that reading about my experiences, along with the opinions of the experts, will give you some tricks to whip out the next time something springs (or squishes) on your path.

Stains on Your Shirt! What Would Rob Do?

Stains can happen to anyone. But for me they seem to happen much more often than for other people. Maybe it's because I dare to eat without a napkin. Maybe it's because of my tendency to consume food and beverages in a more relaxed, reclining position. Or maybe it's just because I'm the kind of guy who likes to talk with his hands, even if those hands happen to be holding a glass of red wine or a hot dog smothered in ketchup.

Over the years, I've spoiled many a shirt and tie, and sadly, even a new pair of Prada pants that I got from Neiman Marcus Last Call for an amazing discount. What were once my pants of pride became my scarlet-stained slacks of shame. Not only was I humiliated, but when I got home and couldn't get the stain out, my clumsiness ended up costing me some good money.

It doesn't have to be like that. I've discovered a few tricks you can use before you go out, or right when the stain hits you, as well as what to do when you get home, that will help combat those annoying accidents.

The first thing you want to do is to pick out your outfit carefully. White suede would be perfect for a Guns N' Roses theme party, but wouldn't a cut-off black T-shirt also be appropriate? The point being, try to find ways to avoid fabrics that can be easily ruined by stains. Stay away from suede, silk, and any type of fabric they make ties out of these days.

What's the easiest fabric to get something out of? White cotton. This is because you always have the option of bleaching it. When I was a waiter one summer, each night I would come home with the nastiest stains all over my white button-down shirt. After a while I didn't even bother washing it, I just bleached it each night. Even though the fabric eventually disintegrated, this strategy saved me hours in the laundry room.

Another tip is to try to avoid certain foods and drinks. The aptly named Christopher White, technical director at America's Best Cleaners (an organization of high-end dry cleaners), says the worst stains are from things like wine and mustard. He also said that compound stains, like coffee with cream and sugar, can be really tricky. Each element has to be treated differently, making removal all the more difficult.

Say you are unable to avoid drinking wine or a cappuccino and you get a stain. What should you do then? What you do in the first few seconds could very well determine the fate of your article of clothing. Chris White says the first thing you want to do is blot with a dry napkin. Soak up as much of the liquid as possible before it can really set—blot, don't rub. Then try cold water. Don't use anything like Sprite or tonic water; their sugar content could create a chemical reaction on your shirt and make things worse. Salt is also out. White explained that stain removal is a science, and that a good dry cleaner will know the chemical components of various stains and how they react with different fabrics and dyes. One other tip I learned from Glenn O'Brien, *GQ*'s style guy, is that vodka works well on red wine stains (though he didn't specify whether it had to be top shelf or a well brand would suffice).

There are some stain-removal products on the market that can be effective in getting out blemishes. Wine Away (which Anna carried with her on our wedding night), is supposed to instantly make wine stains disappear like magic. There are also products like Shout Wipes or the Tide to Go stick for instant stain relief. When using any of these products, read the fine print. These purported lifesavers often offer no guarantees of working, and when dealing with different chemicals, you could exacerbate the problem instead of fixing it.

If you're lucky, you'll have minimized your stain by blotting the errant liquid before it has had time to really soak into your fabric. And if you're *really* lucky, the liquid hasn't landed right on your crotch. (If it has, you probably want to remain seated as much as possible for the rest of the night.) The real work for stain removal usually comes when you get home. You could pretreat the stain with something like Totally Toddler Nursery Stain Remover, which works on spitup as well as on strained peas or any other mushy food you could imagine. You could also soak it in detergent before washing, but as Chris White advocates, it's best to leave the worst blemishes to the pros, who have an arsenal of stain removal techniques to get at the toughest stains. Some of the really high-end cleaners may charge you upwards of fifty dollars for just one nasty stain, but given the prices of designer labels these days, it's probably worth it so you won't have to buy a new pair of Prada pants.

There are a couple of things you should know before entering any dry cleaning establishment. First, choose wisely. If you're the kind of person who likes expensive clothes, you want to find a place that knows what they're doing. Ask around, do some research on dry cleaners before you hand over your valuable threads. Chris White recommends checking out the Web site of America's Best Dry Cleaners to see which of their members are in your area, but you can also check with the Better Business Bureau to find a reputable establishment near you.

Next, it's important that you clearly communicate with the cleaners about your stains. They need to know where the stains are, what they consist of, and most important, whether you've already attempted to pretreat them. Finally, test out your personal comfort level with the dry cleaner—especially important if you need to fess up to stains involving bodily fluids. You don't necessarily have to go through and point out every skid-marked pair of silk boxers you leave at the dry cleaners, but offering a warning is very much appreciated. White says a little note that says "beware" or "handle with gloves" goes a long way toward ingratiating yourself with someone who now knows many of your more intimate secrets.

Of course, some stains can't be conquered by even top-tier dry cleaners. That's when you need to embrace the stain and give it some friends. Your shirt can be repurposed as a garage rag or a smock for painting, or maybe it's now the perfect candidate for being tie-dyed. Then again, if tie-dye is part of your wardrobe, you might not be the kind of person who fusses much over stains to begin with.

Stepped in Dog Poop? What Would Rob Do?

Is there really no better "dang!" moment than when you step in dog poop? The worst part of this dirty predicament is that the revelation of animal excrement on your shoe often doesn't come until long after the treads have been brimming with doo-doo. It's usually when you find yourself in an enclosed space that it hits you—say, after you've just walked across an expensive Persian rug in your aunt's living room. You get that feeling in your gut, that "Oh no, I think I might have stepped in dog poop" feeling. You do a quick shoe check, and if you're lucky, maybe you are wearing flat-soled shoes that are easy to wipe clean. If you have poor luck, as I do, you are probably wearing a brand-new pair of hiking boots, the ones with the deep treads perfect for poop to fill up every little last crevice. What do you do? You can try cleaning it out with a stick if you can find one. Some lucky people, like moms, may have baby wipes nearby, and if you're a proctologist, you may have some spare rubber gloves in your pocket. Most likely you're going to have to do it by hand. Yes, you will have to touch the dog poop with your bare hands. It's so gross.

The sad truth is that I have a large collection of dog-poop experiences. To be sure, some of my *schnauzer shizer* stories are more memorable than others. One that comes to mind happened at my Hebrew elementary school, where I went by my Hebrew name, Elihu. Most people get it confused with Eliahu, a prophet who's ritually invited into Jewish homes during Passover. I can assure you that after my little misstep, nobody was leaving the door open for me. I was outside with the other kids, running through piles of autumn leaves with reckless abandon. Lots of fun, but the leaves camouflaged the mushy land mine that I had unknowingly plopped my little foot into.

Once we settled back into our seats in the classroom, it wasn't long before I heard a loud "*Oy vey!*" My Hebrew school *mora* (teacher), a small, round woman with a red face, looked like she was about to collapse. The smell seemed to hit her and everyone in the room at the same time. We were consumed by the odor. Then she barked out the order: "Everyone check your shoes." I could hear wee voices cry out *lo* (which means *no* in Hebrew). I peeked at one shoe and was relieved to find it untarnished. And then when I lifted up the other one, there it was! A perfect dollop of brown soft-serve mush. It had even picked up a few leaves and twigs along the way. I looked behind me and saw a trail of brown footprints that led right to my desk. It didn't take long for the *mora* to notice the look of terror on my face. "Elihu, go to the bathroom and clean it off right now!"

I took off my shoe and did that unbalanced walk you do when you have one shoe on and one shoe off. I retraced my doody tracks out the door and made a beeline for the bathroom. When I got there, I tried to get out the poop with toilet paper, but it just fell apart in my hands. I then went to paper towels, which got about 80 percent of it. Running the sole of the shoe directly under the faucet got the other 20 percent. Of course, at that age my faucet skills weren't what they are today, so when I put my shoe back on, it made my sock all hot and soggy. To add to the indignity, my shoe squeaked when I walked, serving as an audible reminder of what I'd done.

I have long wondered if there was a better way to recover from this situation, so I sought some professional help. But who would be an expert in this field? A veterinarian? A kennel owner? A dog breeder? Sure, they all deal with dogs on a daily basis, but does that really make them dog-poop *experts*? That's when I came across an industry that I didn't even know existed: professional dog-poop removers. Sounds serious, right? Well, unlike the tough-guy images of industrial waste removal companies, the people in this line of work like to poke fun at their occupation. Among the names of businesses I found were Turds Away, Doodie Free, and Wholly Crap Pet Waste Removal. I got in touch with the good people at Doody Calls, an outfit based in Northern Virginia.

The company was started by Jacob D'Aniello, along with his then girlfriend Susan. He started scooping the yards of his neighborhood after he got home from his day job as an IT consultant, "in a tie and khakis," as he recalled. He soon found there were enough clients for both him and Susan to do it full-time. He told me the two of them would scoop for twelve hours and be exhausted at the end of the day. It doesn't exactly sound like a romantic way to spend time with your girlfriend, but Susan must not have minded, because the two are now married and still in the business together.

In addition to being an expert in unorthodox courtship tactics, Jacob is also very well versed in the art of extracting wayward dog poop. First, he suggests that before you even leave your house, you should be conscious of the weather. A hot summer day not only melts ice cream, it can also turn what was once a hard turd into a lump of mush just waiting to be smashed underfoot. He also says it's helpful to know your neighborhood dogs. If the family next to you has a Saint Bernard or a Great Dane, you have to figure there are bound to be some mega-poops in your vicinity. If the neighbors just have Shih Tzus and Chihuahuas, you probably don't need to be quite so cautious.

I would add that it helps to know your vegetation. When I was growing up, my family dog Biscuit had a favorite patch of lawn that she liked to poop on. My mother used to remark how the grass always seemed to be particularly dense in that section. So look for random patches of thick vegetation and stay away from them. And no matter where you are, look down at the ground as you walk. It might seem obvious, but these days you have to be on guard.

Still, given the sheer size of the American pet population, sooner or later you're going to step into a squish. What then? D'Aniello says his crew has a whole assortment of tools they use to scrape poop out. Despite the obvious frustrations of having boots with deep grooves in them, he intentionally opts for the deep treads because they provide him with the extra traction he needs. If you think about it, the only thing worse than stepping in poop is slipping and falling in it. So if you're worried about slippage and you're in a likely environment—say, picnicking in a park where people let their dogs run around off the leash—you might want to consider leaving home flat-soled sneakers like Vans or Chucks. Also, don't wear flip-flops, because you run the risk of poop getting on your toes . . . or worse, under your toenails. If that doesn't define gag-your-face disgusting, I don't know what does.

Now back to the treatment methods. D'Aniello told me the most effective substance is indeed water. His crew often uses a power washer to quickly blast out the mutt manure. The key here is to keep water from getting inside your shoes, to prevent those soggy soles.

If you discover the mess too late and have already dragged it across your Hebrew school floor or an elegant Persian rug, D'Aniello says a product called Nature's Miracle is the only thing that can save you. It's made up of an enzyme that actually eats up the poop! According to the product's Web site, this stuff "liquefies and neutralizes the stain," unlike soap and water, which can leave unseen remnants of excrement in the fabric. D'Aniello says any trace of dung actually attracts other animals to the area and signals to them that, "Hey, this is a great place to drop a load!" In short, it invites a poop free-for-all, which I don't think you want inside your house.

Now that I'm more knowledgeable on the physics and chemistry of dog poop, I'm considering donating a new power washer and a five-gallon bucket of Nature's Miracle to my old Hebrew school in the hopes that I can spare some innocent little boy (*yeled*) or girl (*yalda*) from suffering the same shameful fate as me. I just hope that stuff is kosher.

Stuck in an Elevator? What Would Rob Do?

I'm lucky not to have many phobias. I'm good with bugs, heights, and darkness; flying on airplanes is no big deal for me, either. I have to say, though, despite conquering some of my earlier feelings of claustrophobia, I still have some lingering fear of being trapped in an elevator. Maybe it's all those movies I've seen where someone gets stuck in an elevator, then escapes by crawling up a shaft, only to face a dramatic shoot-out with an unseen enemy. Even though it's highly unlikely this will happen to me, I still find myself patting my pants pocket just to double-check that my cell phone is there when those elevator doors close. I've also been known to take extra notice of the elevator's emergency system to see if the emergency phone is working.

Luckily, my fear extends only to entrapment, not death. For this I thank Mr. Elisha Otis, who in 1853 invented the safety device that prevents an elevator free-fall should the cable break. Today, Otis is the largest elevator company in the world, and thus the right people to speak to about how worried I should be. Edith DiFrancesco, vice president for Safety and Quality at Otis North and South America, told me that "vertical transportation" in an elevator is really one of the safest ways to travel. My own research confirmed that you are many times less likely to be injured in an elevator than you are in a car, or a plane, or a train, or even on an escalator. (I couldn't find any statistics comparing elevators to monorails.)

Even if Otis says elevators are extremely safe, I still don't like the boxed-in feeling I get from riding certain elevators, like the ones found in old New York City apartment buildings. I'm talking about the platform elevator where you pull a cage door shut and depress a big black button really hard, or manually hold down a lever while you peer out at each floor as you pass it by. It's never a good thing if I end up feeling like I'm the one operating the elevator. The car lurches upward at an uneven pace, and I find myself just waiting for it to choke at any second, which by the way would give me the twisted satisfaction of confirming my pessimism.

Elevator companies know that there are people like me out there. That's the whole reason for the DOOR CLOSE button. Even though in most elevators this button does absolutely nothing, it still provides passengers with a false sense of control while they are being shot up a seventy-five-story skyscraper. Another technique for passenger pacification is the onboard entertainment certain elevators provide. It started with Muzak—bad instrumental

versions of your favorite pop songs that are supposed to calm
your nerves, though the practice of piping in Muzak has been
defunct for quite some time. A newer concept that's gaining popularity is "elevator TV." A company called Captivate
Network (which sounds too much like "Captive Network" for
my taste) now provides programming for elevator passengers.
While this may be another source of ad revenue, I don't know
how much it will do for the claustrophobes who fear the steel
beast that ascends and descends day and night.

Every time there's a major power outage, there are always
some unfortunate members of the populace who find themselves
stuck in an elevator. I found one of these unlikely souls to talk to
about the experience. Deborah Henson-Conant happened to get
in an elevator moments before the power went out. If her name
sounds familiar to you, it's probably because she's a Grammy-
nominated musician who plays a hip harp, which is a small
strap-on harp. (Yeah, that's right, she plays a strap-on.) While
on tour in Texas, she and her partner Jonathan were trapped in
an elevator in San Antonio for three hours. The escape hatch
wasn't an option, since by law, escape hatches are locked from
the outside, which makes sense, because they are really meant
for rescuers to get in, not for people to climb out.

Deborah's elevator ordeal lasted longer than most
because her elevator was not equipped with a call box. Edith
DiFrancesco of Otis said that, had they been trapped in an
Otis elevator, the call box would have connected them to
an Otis operator, who not only would have sent help, but
also would have kept Deborah calm while she waited. If
you aren't completely freaking out in a stalled elevator, the
operator could at least keep you company if you're bored.
Deborah didn't seem to miss the call box. Instead of screaming and shouting for help, she and Jonathan decided to sing

every song they knew. I'm imagining they sang "Message in a Bottle" by the Police or "Help!" by the Beatles.

Now, what would I do? Push the DOOR OPEN button first. I know it sounds too easy to really work, but it's an actual recommendation from Otis. Ultimately, if I am stuck in an elevator, I'm going to try to take advantage of the time I have there, get to know the people around me, maybe engage them in a game of Truth or Dare, or sing some songs the way Deborah and Jonathan did. You never know when befriending your elevator comrades will come in handy. If you discover you need to use the restroom, you could ask their assistance in prying open the doors. (This practice is strongly discouraged.) If you are alone in the elevator, you'll have to simmer in your own thoughts. If your cell phone works, of course call for help; but while you're waiting for the cavalry, isn't this the perfect time to catch up with some old friends, or have that heart-to-heart with your dad that you've been delaying for a while? If all else fails, try sitting in the corner, closing your eyes, and imagining that you're somewhere else, like on a Zen retreat. When else are you going to have this much time for self-reflection?

Speeding Tickets: What Would Rob Do?

It's hard to find a more stomach-churning experience than looking into your rearview mirror and seeing the flashing lights of a cop car behind you. For a split second, you contemplate hitting the gas, but then you remember the countless police chases you've seen on *COPS* and realize that outrunning that squad car probably won't work. You pull over, hoping that the cop caught you going only ten miles over the speed limit and not forty, which you might have been doing five minutes earlier. If you're a guy, you have little chance of winning the officer over by unbuttoning the top button on your shirt, so you need something clever to say. You have only that minute or two as the officer methodically strolls up to your car to prepare. When he or she taps on your car window with that black leather glove, it's go time. The stakes are high here—fouling this up could mean a nasty fine and possibly a huge hit to your monthly car insurance bill.

To get more insight into what cops are thinking, I spoke with Officer Umberto Jimenez of the California Highway Patrol. And yes, that's CHiPs, but no, he doesn't personally know Ponch (I'll get to that in chapter 5). Jimenez warns potential offenders that being a smooth talker won't get you anywhere. He says the majority of instances when you're pulled over result from the simple fact that the officer believes your actions were a danger to other motorists. He adds that every officer—whether a rookie or a longtime vet—has heard it all. In fact, there are a number of cop Web sites and blogs out there, such as AutoCult .com, where cops chat about the all-time worst excuses they've ever heard, such as: "I have to go to the bathroom," "I'm running out of gas," "My speedometer is broken," "My girlfriend just dumped me," or "I'm not wearing my glasses so I couldn't read the speedometer." (FYI, that last one really has no shot at working.)

In my lifetime, I've gotten pulled over about five or six times. I've always been polite and until very recently have never talked my way out of a ticket. My first mistake was to think that cops appreciate the line, "What seems to be the problem, officer?" They don't. Also, "I guess the speed just got away from me" doesn't really work well, especially when you're bombing down California's Pacific Coast Highway with your convertible top down and the music blaring. The only thing that seemed remotely appreciated was an apology. While that might have made my transaction more pleasant, the result was still the same: a big fat ticket. I lived in Los Angeles for five years and wound up taking online traffic school three times. I'm pretty much a pro at the California drivers' exam at this point.

While the United States has no "speed limitless" roads like Germany's Autobahn, a lot of Western states have vast open roads perfect for putting the pedal to the metal. For instance, Arizona, Colorado, Montana, Idaho, and New Mexico all have stretches of highway with a maximum speed limit of seventy-five miles per hour. If you head to Texas, parts of I-10 and I-20 allow you to travel up to eighty miles per hour. But then again, for those five extra miles per hour, you have to ask yourself if it's really worth having a potential run-in with a Texas Ranger. I know I don't need a Chuck Norris wannabe sizing me up.

There are countless gizmos out there that supposedly help you see the cop before he sees you. The most popular is the radar detector, which beeps wildly if it senses radar guns nearby. Unfortunately radar is used almost everywhere these days, and not just by the police. Many photo-enforced stoplights use radar to nab motorists running a red. In addition, ambulances and construction crews use radar to try to get nearby motorists to slow down. Radar detectors can be helpful, but frantically scanning the roadside every time that little thing beeps is not what I consider a fun driving experience. One other note: radar detectors are illegal in my current residence of Washington, D.C., as well as in neighboring Virginia.

Other tricks I've seen to avoid being picked up are dangling a CD in the rearview mirror, which supposedly scrambles radar signals. You can also get a vanity license plate that's a series of

Os and zeros or eights and Bs, which is thought to make it that much harder for an officer to get a good read on your plates as you speed away in your Lamborghini . . . or in your Dodge Caravan, as the case may be.

None of the gadgets, special plates, or speedy rides means a thing once you *are* pulled over. Policemen are generally less sympathetic if they think you don't respect them, or if they think you're trying to outsmart them. If you have a radar detector, shove it under your seat before the cop gets to your car.

What works best is to act as penitent as possible. Remember, they're cops; they joined the force because they like being in a position of authority. Go with the flow and stroke their ego. Say something like, "Yes, Officer," or "I'm so sorry, Officer," or "I feel so bad, Officer." These responses might garner some leniency (or might not, as in my case). My older brother, Mike, goes one step further and works the tear ducts. Not every man can cry on cue—that takes years of experience—but if you've ever seen my brother drive, you'd know he has plenty of that. Crying may be the ultimate in self-emasculation, but judging by Mike's near-spotless driving record, it's clearly effective.

If you can't be moved to tears, consider one police online message board I read where a cop wrote in to say, "I hate it when they don't try to at least come up with something. At least tell me a lie, be creative, make me laugh and I'll probably let you go." The few times my audacious friends have tried the humorous approach, it's actually worked. Just ask my buddy who got out of a speeding ticket by telling the officer *he* was in labor.

From Officer Jimenez's point of view, cops are more concerned about keeping the roads safe than with making a ticket quota. I realized if I could convince police officers that I, too, was safety conscious, maybe I could work my way out of a ticket. It wasn't long after I moved to D.C. that I got to test this theory. I was driving along a stretch of roadway in my shiny black convertible roadster (Mike advised me to get it). I was near the Kennedy Center, where the lanes switch over during rush hour to lead out of the city. Feeling somewhat giddy about driving on the left side British-style, I gave the car a wee bit more gas than was necessary.

At the end of this little stretch was a cop standing outside his car with a radar gun pointing right at me. He motioned with his finger for me to pull over, and I followed it like a tractor beam to a parking lot where two other cars were waiting for their punishment. All I could think about in my head was the word "safety." It was like those Men Without Hats lyrics: "Ssss . . . Aaaa . . . Ffff . . . Eeee . . . Tttt . . . Yyyy." I told the cop I was unaware of the speed limit—which didn't go over well—but then I talked to him about the lane change and how I was "unsure of how it was going, so I just followed the guy in front of me." (It was him, not me!) Then I added, "I'm awfully sorry, Officer. It's just that I'm not familiar with this road and was just concentrating on the road and being safe so I didn't notice the speed limit sign!" At this I received a sigh and a look of understanding. He came back and gave me a piece of paper I will cherish for many years to come: my first written warning. I was so excited, I nearly peeled out of the parking lot.

Stuck in the Middle Seat of an Airplane? What Would Rob Do?

Air travel can be brutal. Parking lots are miles away from terminals, there are long lines at check-in, and even longer lines to get through security. By the time you get to your gate, you're already exhausted. When you get on the plane, forget about having an empty seat next to you so you can stretch out. Nowadays airlines need to squeeze every dime they can out of every flight, so your chances are better than ever of getting that loathsome middle seat.

The middle seat stinks for a lot of reasons. You have neither the comfort of easy bathroom access nor the view from the window. You're wedged in, and depending on how long your flight is, you have to tolerate not one but two potentially annoying strangers on either side of you. Being in the middle seat means pretending you're completely comfortable sitting inches away from people who may be talking your ear off, crowding your personal space, or inundating you with flatulence for hours on end.

It was never even a question that I, as the youngest of three children, would get the middle seat on the plane when our family traveled somewhere. On one side would be my snoring brother with his face smushed up against the window blocking the view. On the other side would be my sister barricading my path to the aisle and freedom. She'd be game for a few rounds of gin rummy before nodding off, leaving me alone to try to bend over to reach the bag of "vacation candy" at my feet without smashing my head into the fully reclined seat in front of me. People in the middle always seem to recline to eke out whatever extra room they can.

I figured my days of "middleseatdom" would finally be over when I became the leader of my own flock. That was not to be the case. It's been made clear to me that my role as the head of the household is to make sure that my wife is comfortable at all times. So in movie theaters, at concerts and sporting events, and on airplanes, Anna always gets the aisle.

I guess I should have read the fine print of our marriage contract a little better.

As you can see, my middle seat credentials are fully in order. Now I'll let you in on what I've learned from David Grossman, a former airline industry executive who writes a business travel column for *USA Today*, on what insiders do to avoid the "hump from hell."

To avoid the middle seat, Grossman suggests going on standby for your own flight. It's a risky move, since you'll be one of the last to board the plane and your overhead baggage compartment may be full. If you have only a small carry-on, then you may be in luck; otherwise, you'll have to check your bag. The reason to go standby, Grossman says, is that the seats that are free for standby passengers are often the very best ones on the plane; the passengers who originally occupied them are usually the ones who paid full price and have been upgraded to even better seats. (A quick side note: going standby at "will call" is also a great way to get really good seats at a theater or a sporting event. Venues often hold premier seats for last-minute VIP requests. This is how I once got sixth row center seats at a sold-out show of *The Lion King* in London, the one place I didn't mind squeezing into a middle seat.)

You may also want to factor in the type of aircraft you're booking your reservation on. Grossman points out how each aircraft has what the industry calls its own "pitch," or space, in between seats. Web sites such as SeatGuru.com or SeatExpert .com will help you figure out which airplanes have the most leg room. After searching economy class seat pitch charts on SeatGuru.com, I found that Finnair's Boeing 757-200s have a paltry pitch of just twenty-eight to twenty-nine inches, while United Boeing 757s have a seat pitch of thirty-six inches. That's a full eight more inches for your knees. You can look up seat width, too. The winner in that category is US Airways Beech 1900, whose economy-class seat is nineteen inches wide. That's pretty good, considering that the average width on most first-class flights is around twenty-one inches.

Another trick I've heard about is to ask at the counter if you can sit in a row where there are people with the same last name. There's a good chance this row was reserved by a family who paid for a window and an aisle, then crossed their fingers that the middle would be free. If you sit there, you'll foil their plans, and most likely one of them will slide over next to the other one, so you won't be in between them.

Let's say you end up in that middle seat despite your best efforts. There are some things you can do to preserve your sanity and your space. The first is to defend your leg room. There's a device called the Knee Defender that makes it impossible for the seat in front of you to recline. While many claim it works great, I could see it leading to a confrontation. Can you just imagine the person in front of you screaming, "Hey, you bastard, did you just lock my seat?" It seems evil to tamper with another person's seat, especially since I'm a firm believer in seat-reclining karma. As I already mentioned, middle seat people seem to be the first to recline their chairs out of some spiteful vengeance for their crummy location. Fortunately, there seems to be an unwritten code of the skies that for flights under two hours, most people don't bother reclining their seatbacks. I like to think that if I'm courteous enough not to recline my chair on a short flight, karma will reward me with a person in front of me who respects my leg room. There are a few exceptions to my "no reclining on short flights" rule. Obviously, it's okay to go for it if nobody's behind you, or if there's a small child who doesn't need the leg room (though you might be in for a lot of kicking). Lastly, if the person behind you has reclined themselves, give it right back to them and recline away.

If karma isn't working, I try to protect my space by offering some subtle resistance the second I see the seat in front of me start to move down. I engage my own knee lock against the seatback, holding it up while a big Schwarzenegger-like vein pops out of my head. The other method is to use the "head block," where you lean over like you're having a really bad day and use your forehead to resist any reclining (watch out for recliners who use a jerking motion to get their seats back, as this move could lead to some head trauma). But despite your best efforts, a reclining seat will sometimes catch you off guard. When that happens, get up to go to the bathroom, then grab the seat in front of you. Act like you're trying to steady yourself because of turbulence and use the opportunity to shove that seatback into the upright position. They'll never know what hit them.

Once you've secured your leg room, you'll want to protect your space from the other passengers in your row. For some tips on this, I spoke with Mike Davidson, a blogger and CEO of Newsvine.com, an online amalgamator of different news sources. I found out about Davidson when I stumbled upon one of his blog posts divulging his own middle-seat survival secrets. He says it's important to quickly establish yourself on the armrest. As the middle passenger, either you can go for outright dominance, or you can work your elbows onto the back end of the armrest, letting your neighbors occupy the front part with their forearms. Now, for me, wrist jockeying gets into some pretty dicey territory, because the last thing you want is to wind up having continuous physical contact with a stranger over the course of several hours. One thing I do is wear a jacket as sort of a flesh guard between me and the skin of other passengers. The best kind of jacket for the job is a big down ski jacket, which creates a huge puffy buffer zone. If you get hot, you can take it off and leave it wrapped around you. Now it's a makeshift cocoon, insulating you from the other passengers.

The only time being in the middle seat can be a bonus is if your better half is occupying the seat next to you. You won't need that puffy jacket to block anyone out, but it will make an ideal pillow when you try to establish what I call "sleeping supremacy." This is where the first person who dozes off gets to sleep on the other. I'm not talking quaint "head on shoulder" sleeping—I'm talking "raised armrest, full face planted in the lap of the other person" type sleeping. Wouldn't you know that airplane trips have a way of inducing a narcoleptic reaction in Anna? She's usually asleep before we reach cruising altitude. But that's okay. I've also discovered that if I let her get some extra sleep on the plane, I can totally guilt her into letting me sleep in the next time our daughter wakes up at three in the morning. "Hey honey, you've got this one, right?"

If you happen to be flying solo and find yourself hating life in the middle seat, my last piece of advice is not to be a poor sport about it. Whether through money, thinking ahead, or plain chicanery, your row-mates figured out how not to be you, and they don't want to hear your sad story. They're most likely intentionally stymieing any banter in fear that you're going to be *that* guy who talks someone's ear off on a twelve-hour flight. Don your blackout eye shades, put on your headphones, and go through the playlist you made for this flight (mine includes the bands Air, Air Supply, and Jefferson Airplane). Better yet, pop a sleeping pill and put yourself out of your misery. As a last resort, try chatting up the person directly *behind* you. If you haven't reclined your seat, they'll most likely be friendly.

2
.
Wooing Woes

When it came to the ladies, I used to think I was hot stuff. Maybe it was having cool older siblings who helped me feel confident, or maybe I had an inflated sense of my smooching skills, but whatever the reason, I've been chasing after lasses from the time I could walk. When all the other boys thought girls had cooties, I was angling for position during naptime to get a prime spot next to the cute redhead.

In elementary school, my fascination with the opposite sex only increased. I spent afternoon recess chasing girls, trying to give them kisses. A girl named Carey in first grade figured out that if she smiled at me, I'd "do underdoggies" for her on the swing set during recess. Despite how perverse "doing underdoggies" sounds, it's actually just the act of pushing someone so high on the swings that you can run underneath them. When all I got from Carey were smiles and not kisses, it didn't take long for me to wise up and move on.

High school was the same routine, bopping around from girl to girl in my class, but by then I was interested in a little bit more than just handholding and cheek kissing. I became famous for what my sister dubbed the "Rob Sachs everything date." A typical everything date would include lunch, followed by miniature golf, then a movie around four o'clock, then dinner, a stop for ice cream cones on the way home, and then we'd watch a video in my basement. The basement was where I usually attempted to go for it. My parents were strict about not letting girls go in my bedroom, but they were surprisingly cool about that basement. It was an unwritten rule that they didn't bother us down there—something I could have used to my advantage, had I not completely exhausted every girl I got down there from the everything date. Most girls just fell asleep. Too bad Red Bull didn't exist back then.

In college and throughout my twenties, I finally began to widen my dating circle to include people I didn't know from school. That's when I started noticing real deficiencies in my dating skills. How I dressed, how I danced—even knowing what movie to pick on a date—all suddenly took on greater significance. While I usually could charm my way through mishaps like kissing a girl on the nose instead of the lips, there were times I wished I had known a little more.

This chapter includes what I've learned, along with some real insider stuff from people who *know* romance. I've talked to everyone from a Hollywood director who specializes in romantic comedies, to a real-life matchmaker, to Italy's gift to the world of sexiness, Fabio Lanzoni. I even throw in an expert at carnival games, in case you need an extra boost in proving your manliness. Lastly, when you're ready to seal the deal and drop the "love bomb" on your lady, I explain how the right song can be your best wingman. I talked to two legendary bands on how to put together a great romantic playlist and how to write the perfect love song.

The one thing this chapter doesn't cover is marital tips. It's not that there aren't indignities associated with being married, it's that I'm finding that after only a few years of being joined in holy matrimony, the advice is always the same: No matter what, your wife is always right. Until you take that vow, you actually get to have a say in some of what goes on in your love life. I hope that this chapter will help you maximize this fleeting power.

Avoiding a Chick Flick: What Would Rob Do?

When I think about the worst movie I've ever picked for a date, the one that instantly comes to mind is *The Celebration*, or perhaps you're more familiar with its Danish title, *Festen*. This movie came out when I was studying abroad in London for a semester (see "American in London? What Would Rob Do?" in chapter 5), and I was determined to see as many foreign films as I could (bad idea). The date was with a girl who lived on my hall (another very bad idea). The movie was supposed to be a formality, since I already knew we'd be going home together at the end of the night.

The Celebration starts off nicely enough, with grown-up siblings returning to their parents' house for their father's sixtieth birthday. It's all very "festive" until about fifteen minutes in, when the son accuses dear old dad of raping both him and his sister—who, by the way, had just committed suicide. Hijinks ensue. I slunk so far down in my chair, my back was sticking to the candy on the floor by the end of the movie. Needless to say, no nookie that night.

The best date movies are, of course, the ones that you only really see half of because you start making out as soon as the lights dim. Oh yeah! Can I get a high five!?! (Do people really make out in theaters anymore? I think stadium seating has made this endeavor a lot more of a technical challenge.)

Over the years, I've made many aimless laps around video stores searching for that perfect mixture of action, romance, and comedy that would be both appealing to me and endearing to her. Being a child of the '80s, I've always had a soft spot for Brat Pack films with superstars of the decade like Anthony Michael Hall, Judd Nelson, and Molly Ringwald. My favorite is *The*

Breakfast Club, followed closely by *Sixteen Candles*. I desperately wanted to talk to John Hughes, who wrote these movies as well as the amazing *Ferris Bueller's Day Off*, but Mr. Hughes was hard to reach at the time and, sadly, has now passed on. Thankfully, John Hughes's protégé Howie Deutch was willing to talk to me about what makes a great date movie.

Deutch got his big break directing another Brat Pack film, *Pretty in Pink*, then went on to direct the great romantic comedy *Some Kind of Wonderful*. In 2008, he directed the Dane Cook film *My Best Friend's Girl*. Deutch said the secret to a great date movie is to have "sentiment without erring on the side of sentimentality," something that Deutch himself admitted to having done in the past. A lot of romantic comedies are flat-out cheesy. You wind up being so embarrassed to be sitting in the theater that you want to put a paper bag over your head while watching it, so nobody knows you've actually forked over good money to see this lousy film. But chances are your date won't be cowering next to you, since in my experience, women tend to have a much higher threshold for romantic cheesiness than guys. That said, date movies shouldn't be a test of your endurance, unless you owe your date one because the last movie you picked was *The Celebration*.

The problem is, it's hard to figure out which movies are worth seeing, since romantic comedies tend to be hit-or-miss. The way trailers are cut these days, a winner like *When Harry Met Sally* can look identical to a bomb like *How to Lose a Guy in 10 Days*. Usually it's helpful if you have an established comedian in the movie, but that's never a guarantee. Robin Williams may be a funny man, but *License to Wed* was not funny. Perhaps a hot girl can save a film? Yes, but eye candy gets boring after a while. Jessica Simpson may be cute, but she's no fun to watch trying to act. You could also try to find an edgier R-rated

gross-out romantic comedy like Judd Apatow's *Knocked Up* or
The 40-Year-Old Virgin. But now you run the risk of revealing
your stunted sense of humor too early in your relationship.

I turned back to Howie Deutch for some advice on how to
tease out the good from the bad. He passed along some knowledge from another great director, the late Sydney Pollack, who
said that "every movie can be a love story" if viewed under the
right lens. It may be a stretch to find the love story in *Alien vs.
Predator* or *Leatherface: Texas Chainsaw Massacre III*, but his larger
point was that any movie involves a degree of human drama. So
don't be afraid to expand your search for a date movie beyond
the romantic comedy section. One of Deutch's favorite love stories, by the way, is *Rocky*. What an amazing pick!

If your date winds up liking a movie *you* actually enjoy as
well, that should say a lot about the potential for your relationship. Just remember that it's okay to take her to a "guy" movie
if there's an actual story line to it beyond car chases and gun-
fights, and that you should never, ever, pick a foreign or independent film without first thoroughly reading reviews or plot
summaries for any surprise twists. And lastly, when you're in a
jam, pick a classic she's already seen. That way she wouldn't be
mad if you should, you know, "get distracted" for a couple of
scenes here and there.

Making a Great Playlist: What Would Rob Do?

Back when playlists were known as "mix tapes" and were actually recorded onto a tape, creating them involved real-time
dubbing from a dual cassette deck. You could learn a lot about
how much the person liked you, not only from the songs they

picked but by the handwriting on the cassette case insert. How scrupulously did they document the songs? Did they include both the artist and the song title? Were there other little notes hidden on the back? We all know we looked for the secret meaning in the songs that were included, wondering if the selection of a certain love song was a message intended to tell us something more.

Getting a mix tape was a great way of discovering new bands, grooving to classic hits, passing time in the car, or just getting through a late night of studying. The tape itself also had charm in its imperfect production. Sometimes the sound levels would be completely different between songs, or there would be weird seven-second-long gaps, or (my favorite) the last song would just randomly cut out right in the middle of a lyric because the tape ran out.

I used to love receiving mix tapes, not only because I was psyched to hear new music and learn about someone else's musical tastes, but also because I was honored by the sheer fact that someone had taken the time to even make a mix for me. I remember receiving a 120-minute mix tape and being blown away by the effort it must have taken to select all those songs.

Now that technology has replaced the cassette tape, some of the homemade touches of the mix tape have faded away. Computer programs precisely measure out the space available on a CD and ensure a perfect amount of spacing between tracks. Amazon, iTunes, and Rhapsody make finding songs easier than ever. Yet even with all the advances in technology that have occurred, they can't eliminate the biggest remaining danger in making mixes: including the wrong song.

Case in point: "Every Breath You Take" by the Police. Sounds like a romantic song about a guy fawning over every breath his beloved takes? Actually, it could be a scary song about someone stalking you, or about Big Brother watching and trying to control society. Similarly, the peppy "Lust for Life" by Iggy Pop and its candid exploration of drug culture is not necessarily a message you want to pass on to your sweetheart, though that didn't faze Royal Caribbean cruise lines when they used the song in one of their commercials.

There are a few ways I like to get around this problem of lyrics that can be read the wrong way. One way is to pick completely obvious songs, like the Beatles' "I Wanna Hold Your Hand" or Marvin Gaye's "Sexual Healing." There's really no hidden meaning to those songs. The other thing I've done is attach a disclaimer to the CD that informs the listeners "not to read too much into the lyrics." A more radical step is to set up an interview with the musicians you're putting on the mix and ask them point-blank what the heck they meant by their lyrics. That's precisely what I did with the band Squeeze.

You may know Squeeze from their classic hit "Tempted," a catchy tune everyone seems to remember: "Tempted by the fruit of another . . . tempted but the truth is discovered." The band got their start back in London in the 1970s with Chris Difford writing the lyrics and Glenn Tilbrook the music. It's a formula that has worked for over thirty years, though their commercial success peaked in the early 1980s.

I have always liked the Squeeze song called "Pulling Mussels (From the Shell)." I was considering putting it on a mix I was making for my wife, but when I double-checked the lyrics online, I was confused. I had no clue what anything in this song meant. How random is it to be singing about the act of gutting pieces of seafood? They might as well have called it "Slitting Salmon with a Knife."

I asked Difford about it and learned that many of their songs' lyrics are rooted in his own personal history. "Pulling Mussels (From the Shell)" is about a memory he has from his time spent at a British holiday camp, a budget resort type of place that includes basic accommodations, entertainment, and other facilities. That didn't explain the lyric: "In bingo for all the nines, a panda for sweet little niece." I asked Difford straight up where he was going there. "It's just a very English lyric so it's no wonder it trips you up," he said, but he stopped short of translating for me because he felt "the songs should really speak for themselves."

His bandmate Glenn Tilbrook chimed in, "When I read things or listen to songs that have been written about circumstances that I don't know very well, for me, that's a journey that takes me somewhere that I haven't been before. If you don't understand what something means you fill in the blanks yourself. That's part of what your brain does, and I think that's a great journey to go on."

Good enough for me. This song's going on Anna's mix tape, and I hope she'll enjoy coming up with her own version of what it's about. Hopefully that will include positive thoughts about me.

Another problem, though, is comprehending the lyrics in the first place. How many times have you listened to a song and thought, "What did they just say?" It's funny when people make up their own lyrics rather than take the time to read the liner notes (though many bands, like R.E.M., don't include a lyric sheet). Squeeze has a song called "Goodbye Girl" in which they sing about "sunlight on the lino" ("lino" being a very British substitute for the word "linoleum"). Never having heard that term before, I assumed it was the slurring of another word. In my head, I made up the lyric "sunlight on Milano," placing the song in Italy.

I asked Difford what he thought about me singing his song with the wrong lyrics. "Once you've written a song and put it on record," he replied, "it ceases to become your property. You're kind of passing it on and people can take what they will for it." Either he was being incredibly nice about it, or maybe that was an excuse for questionable enunciation.

What Difford does have an ear for is musical flow. When I'm making a mix, I try to vary the tempo so that I don't have a run of five really slow songs in a row. Making a mix is like being a DJ. Even though your recipient could just skip to the next song, you don't want to make a mix that has them skipping a bunch of songs in a row. DJs and bands do this all the time when they're creating set lists. Once on tour, Squeeze found themselves inserting their classic "Black Coffee in Bed" right into the middle of their concert to offset what they perceived as a lull.

While club DJs and bands like Squeeze have the opportunity to change what they play each night and see how the crowd reacts, you only get one shot with the mix. Fortunately, I've figured out a way to gauge my audience before I hand it over to them. I make a mix for myself first. I then play it for my intended recipients when they're over for a visit or when we're out driving in the car. I figure out what songs they liked best and then tweak the mix just for them. Another bonus to taking this approach is that by having them listen to some of the music ahead of time, there's a good chance that one or two of the songs I played for them will already be stuck in their head when I give them their mix. It is an unexpected and much appreciated gift. I find the only way to get a stuck song dislodged is to blast it out by putting it on repeat for about twenty minutes. As Difford would say, once you've tired of the song, you can finally get back to being "all the nines."

At least that's what I think he'd say.

Winning Carnival Games: What Would Rob Do?

I don't know why, but I have always had an obsession with carnivals and fairs. I started out loving just the rides. There was the Roundup, where you're basically in a human salad spinner, those carnival swings where you fly around in a circle on a string tethered to a gigantic spinny thing. And there was another one called Flying Bobs that tosses you around in a circle and then halfway through reverses and throws you in the other direction. Do you see a trend here? I was a kid who loved getting dizzy.

Where I'm from, the biggest fair of the year is the June Fete. It's been going on for decades on some donated farm land in Huntingdon Valley, Pennsylvania. In addition to the rides, the June Fete also boasts a craft show, a petting zoo, a bingo tent, and even classic-car and horse-jumping competitions. But what I always liked the most about the Fete was the midway. I was obsessed with the idea of winning one of those colossal stuffed animals in a game of chance.

My family never missed a June Fete. Apart from my allotment of ride tickets, I'd get five or six dollars for the midway. I'd waste a buck or two trying to toss a ring around the neck of a two-liter Coke bottle. Those stuffed animals hanging above that game must have had beards on them, since I never saw anyone win one. When I got down to my last dollar, I would go back to my tried-and-true game of chance: darts. The game was simple: chuck a dart, pop a balloon, win a prize. Growing up, we had a dartboard in the family basement, so winning this one was never an issue. The problem was, the prizes were usually a rubber snake or a stuffed animal so small you could literally stuff it in your front pocket. A slight variation on the "pop a balloon" game was the "hit a poster" with a dart game. Over the years I acquired an impressive set of '80s hair-band posters. (I also have a couple of "My Little Pony" posters from some errant throws.)

Let's not forget two other things that make fairs fun: the food and the element of surprise. When it comes to fair food, where else can you walk around eating a gigantic turkey leg without looking like a barbarian? It's only at fairs that the calories in a piping-hot funnel cake don't seem to count. These are delicacies to be cherished. I also like cotton candy, but I want mine made fresh from spinning a paper cone around the blowing sugar, not that prepackaged stuff that's been sitting in a plastic bag all day.

As for surprises, it could be anything from seeing farm oddities like an oversize albino pig or a prizewinning duck (who judges these things?) to lawn-mower racing competitions and husband-calling contests (the woman who shouts her husband's name in the loudest and most original way wins). My all-time favorite fair moment came when I was about thirteen. My grandmother was visiting from Manhattan for the weekend, and my parents decided to take everyone to the Great Allentown Fair in Allentown, Pennsylvania. We wandered around until we came upon a large wrestling ring. What I witnessed was a surprise that has been forever seared into my memory—a pair of three-hundred-pound women going head-to-head in a pit of oatmeal! I don't know what I enjoyed more, having ringside seats to the spectacle, or seeing Grandma's reaction to it all.

For many years, I was more than content to go to the fair with my buddies to play games and go on rides. As I got older, I came to rely on the June Fete as a place to take a date. After enduring an awkward car ride with my parents, I'd whisk my lady friend away to the grandeur of the Fete, where I would own the place for the next three hours. I'd work the spinny rides, sure, but after a while I would be called upon to show off my midway skills. With a girl by my side, my manliness was on the line. I could win her a poster, but they always wanted the big stuffed animal. The older I got, the fewer excuses I had for losing. You'd think by a certain age I'd have mastered knocking down those stupid milk bottles from the pedestal. Sadly, this was not the case at the June Fete or any other carnival midway I ventured across.

There was one exception. It was at Six Flags Great Adventure in New Jersey. I encountered a strange game where you had to throw a hula hoop over a big stuffed animal on a square platform. To win you had to ring the animal and fit the hoop perfectly over the square platform. Intrigued, I plunked down a dollar, picked up the ring, and chucked it into the air. Amazingly, I nailed it on the first toss. I was ecstatic! I won a humongous stuffed dog with cutesy big brown eyes. Unfortunately, my female companion was my older sister, Andrea. Eventually that pooch made its way to the attic, where all the other stuffed animals in my family went to die.

Marrying Anna relieved me of any obligation to prove myself at carnivals, but ever since I became a dad I've been feeling that midway pressure mounting again. Since I'm planning to take my daughter to countless fairs in her lifetime, I'm going to have to master the midway anew so I can win her the giant teddy bear.

To help me brush up on my skills, I enlisted the help of Brett Witter, author of *Carnival Undercover*. Witter's book examines all aspects of the carnival, and includes secrets on how to win those midway games of skill. Witter said the easiest way to tell how hard a game is going to be is to look at the prizes.

The harder games have those huge stuffed animals. The ones with the small plush toys are where you'll have a better shot. Witter said you want to be up-front with the operator running the game and ask ahead of time what you win. Sometimes the first prize you win isn't even on display, like a three-cent plastic comb that gets pulled out of a box under the counter. Also watch out for the "trading up" scam, where you easily win one small prize but it takes you three "trade-ins" to get a decent prize. You may end up playing half a dozen games and spending upwards of fifteen dollars for something that's probably not worth two bucks.

Witter said the one game where you have a decent shot of winning a good prize is the basketball shot. It sounds easy, but there are a couple of things carnivals do to put the odds in their favor. The rim is usually placed higher than a standard hoop, and it also may be slightly smaller or oval shaped to make it harder for the ball to go in. In some cases the rim may even be bent or banged up. If something looks fishy, you should ask the guy running the game to demonstrate a shot himself. You should also check out the ball itself. Sometimes they're overinflated, causing them to blast off of the rim or backboard.

Witter said the easiest way to make the basket is to "shoot it underhand, especially with super bouncy balls." It's the good old granny shot, or if you prefer, an imitation of Ollie's famous foul shots in the semifinals from the movie *Hoosiers*. Shooting it underhand takes the velocity off the ball. If you're averse to shooting underhand in front of a crowd and your lady friend, you could opt for the straight swish, but it's a much tougher shot to make.

Another midway game you might have some luck with is the water-pistol race game. This is where people sit down in front of a row of squirt guns, and, after a bell rings, they have to hit the target in front of them, which then propels a horse or blows up a balloon. It's a race to see which balloon pops first. This game is enticing because someone is guaranteed to win each round. Witter said the game is actually won or lost within the first two seconds because it comes down to who is able to hit the target right at the start and hold their stream of water on the target once they hit it. He suggests aiming a skosh high before the game starts because it takes a split second for the water pressure to hit full blast.

In the game where you knock milk bottles off the pedestal, Witter said the trick is to "hit right in the center so that you hit all three at once." When playing a target-shooting game, try to "shoot around the star or shoot a straight line above the star." Finally, I asked Witter about the one game I was dying to know the trick to: the Coke-bottle ring-toss game.

Witter agreed this game is so frustrating because it looks so easy to win. The problem, Witter said, is that people think they can ring a bottle by lobbing one ring at a time, but that never really happens. The only way to get a ring on a bottle is to slow it down or get it to ricochet off one bottle neck onto another. The best way to do this is to *gently* toss a ring and keep it low. An abovehand toss will just cause the ring to bounce off, so try crouching down and doing more of a soft Frisbee toss.

There's one other technique Witter has seen work in the past. It involves throwing four or more rings at once. The rings will make it easier to knock each other onto a bottle. "If they actually hit a bottle," Witter said, "those three may bounce off, but the bottom one will probably stay on." Anna and I tried this technique and had no luck with it, or with a lot of the other games Witter advised us on. The truth is, knowing how to beat the game is great, but it won't get you very far if you're not willing to spend the money to practice the skill set. While I haven't convinced Anna that investing in a BB gun firing range is a wise use of the limited space in our house, there are a bunch of basketball courts near us that I can practice my granny shot on, just as long as nobody's watching.

Surviving on the Dance Floor: What Would Rob Do?

One of the best ways to impress women is with your moves on the dance floor. A great dancer is someone who's full of confidence, flair, and pizzazz. Fred Astaire had it, John Travolta had it, and my personal hero, the late Patrick Swayze, definitely had it, despite the fact that he also had a major mullet.

As for myself, I definitely did not have it. Back in college, I took some dance classes when the movie *Swingers* was popular and people were rediscovering zoot suits and swing music. At frat parties, there would be some really lame couple in their saddle shoes who would clear out an obscenely large section of the dance floor and then twirl around like crazy, flipping each other over their backs. For a brief moment, I wanted to be like those idiots. Fortunately, the few dance steps I had learned in class were forgotten by the time I returned to my dorm room.

As I got older, I realized that having some semblance of competence is useful on the dance floor. Grabbing my date's butt and slinking back and forth only works for two or three songs, max. Sooner or later, you need to learn a few steps. To find out how I could channel some better dance moves, I talked to Ron Montez, a seven-time U.S. Professional Latin Champion dancer. He said confidence is a big factor, but as a pro he also stresses competence. Winging it only goes so far. True confidence comes from knowing what you're doing, meaning you should take some classes and learn a few steps. It doesn't even have to be a big investment—many salsa clubs offer free classes. I tried it, and the only "step" I learned was a very basic pattern—up with your right foot, bring your left foot up together with the right; then step back with your right, and bring back your other foot. This is akin to walking in place. It's amazing, though, how dressing up this step by swinging your arms and putting on a big smile makes you look like you know what you're doing. Getting comfortable with yourself and mastering a few basic steps will go a long way in the nightclub.

Let's say you haven't gotten around to taking classes and you find yourself on the dance floor when the music starts. Don't worry. You can still be passable without having to resort to the Electric Slide you learned back when you were thirteen. Passing as a dancer is a lot more about knowing what not to do rather than worrying too much about how to do something right. Montez told me that the worst sin to commit is being off beat, so start there. Finding the beat is as simple as tapping your foot. If you're tapping in time with the percussion, you've found the beat. If you're in a hip-hop club, just put your hand on a speaker. The beat is that pulsating bass that's making the speaker pop in and out.

Once you've got the beat, you're ready for the most basic of all dance moves—the side-step tap. First, take a step to the left and then bring over your right foot. Then step back to the right and bring over your left foot. The trick is to be stepping side-to-side *with* the beat. Once you have that mastered, you can add your own bit of flair. Shake some imaginary maracas, or get your hips and head to join in the side-to-side motion. Whatever it is, go for it. What you want to avoid is having cement legs. Make

sure you don't keep your feet bolted to the floor. You'll look like
one of those little squeeze toys with the elastic limbs that can only
bend from the waist up. Moving your feet around frees up your
whole body so you can dance more fluidly and naturally. If you
start to panic, find another guy who looks like he knows what he's
doing and try to emulate him. Do it on the sly, though, and avoid
copying the guy dancing right next to you so you don't look like
a choreographed duo.

Montez also said there are a few dance floor no-no's. First,
respect the ladies. In my experience, a woman who wants to
dance with you will signal it by nodding in your direction, or
by grabbing your hand as she sidles up next to you. Don't get
carried away. There's no need to get up behind any woman
and start thrusting your pelvis into her back. Anna confirms
that the overwhelming majority of women do not consider this
kind of aggressiveness to be a turn-on.

Second, respect other people's space in general. There's
no need to be knocking into everyone like a renegade robot.
Find a spot on the floor that gives you ample room to do
your stuff without ruining it for everyone around you. While
you're at it, watch out for your partner, too. I dated a girl
who had a penchant for dancing backward without looking.
I'd wonder where she was going and if I was supposed to follow her, then I'd wince as she knocked into people with her
butt. I called her the backward conga-line dancer. I also once
watched someone twirl herself right into a table full of martinis, which then spilled onto someone's suede coat. (Whoever
invented the martini glass is a genius, because he or she figured out that the person drinking from it will have to order
two or three more to account for everything that spills out of
the glass.) When dancing with a female companion, try to rein
in her wild side so you don't both end up having to pay other

people's dry cleaning bills (see "Stains on Your Shirt! What Would Rob Do?" in chapter 1.)

Finally, don't dance outside your limits. A lot of clubs these days play hip-hop and rap, and there isn't much formal dancing between partners. This is a great time to practice your side-step moves or test out some freestyle rump shaking. If you end up at a salsa club and you don't know the salsa steps, let the other salsa fanatics have their fun. You can only wing it for so long before you'll be called out for the buffoon you really are. Even worse, some guy who *really* knows what he's doing is going to ask your partner to dance with him, and then you'll feel the real humiliation of public emasculation. Trust me, it's not fun.

Cooking a Romantic Meal: What Would Rob Do?

When you're dating someone, at some point eating out every night is a little impractical, not to mention that it takes you farther away from the place you want to wind up anyway—your bedroom. Why not make your special someone a home-cooked meal to show her how much you care?

My foray into cooking started with breakfast. The first things I made were scrambled eggs and French toast, which I learned how to cook watching my mother on Sunday mornings. For a long time, they were the *only* things I knew how to make. When my high school English class had a potluck dinner, I brought scrambled eggs. What I didn't take into account is how eggs need to be served hot, not premade and laid out on a tray. It was sad to watch everyone load up on all the other dishes while my languid eggs sat there all by their lonesome getting cold. Only my buddy Brendan served himself a huge helping of eggs. He didn't eat them, but it was a nice gesture and saved my dish from looking completely untouched.

When I got to college, I decided to learn on my own how to cook something beyond eggs and ramen noodles. I started simple—boiling pasta, cooking chicken breasts in a frying pan, and throwing together ingredients to make a salad. With a little store-bought bread and a bottle of wine, I could whip up a decent meal. Before long, I was ready to invite a lady over for dinner. She was a cute brown-eyed arts major who lived on the same block as me. I had my eye on her all semester and finally mustered up the courage to ask her over.

Really wanting to impress my date, I made pecan pie for dessert. It's a Sachs classic—my mother always made it for special occasions. Mom makes a Kentucky variation called a Derby Pie that's full of chocolate chips and is insanely good. I was convinced that if I could capture some of Mom's magic, I could win this girl over.

I bought a premade pie crust, preheated the oven, and started combining the ingredients from my mom's recipe in the bowl. Eggs, check; sugar, check; chocolate chips, check. When I got to the vegetable oil, I realized I had forgotten to pick up any in the supermarket. I looked around the house but could find only extra virgin olive oil. Hmmm, well, I figured since olives were a vegetable and it was oil, how different could it be? I dumped it in and popped my pie in the oven.

My dinner of chicken breasts and pasta was going really well and I couldn't wait to unveil my pecan pie. I should have known something was amiss when I was serving it, because it was really too goopy and looked nothing like my mother's creation. Confident in my baking powers, I forged ahead. This was my big mistake. My poor date literally gagged when she put the first bite in her mouth. Disaster had struck. What I should have realized was that cooking and baking are two very different things. It's good to be a little creative and wing it with your frying pan, but the oven is a more precise instrument. Like chemistry, baking should be done with a safety-first attitude. You may have oven mitts, but in my case protective goggles and a fire extinguisher should have been on hand as well.

These days, I find myself in the kitchen more than ever. The era of "Honey, what's for dinner?" is gone. In my house, we split up the tasks, and that often puts me in front of the stove. For some expert advice, I contacted Rocky Fino, author of *Will Cook for Sex*. Not only does his cookbook have a great title, but he also shares a name with the greatest Philadelphia sports figure of all time (excluding Mike Schmidt, Bobby Clarke, and Dr. J).

Fino insisted that you have to work with good ingredients. Take your time at the supermarket and buy quality meats and vegetables. Otherwise, you're at a disadvantage before you even start cooking. I personally think farmers' markets are a great place to find top-notch produce, though I always come home with random stuff. Fino said that while fancier stores like Whole Foods cost more, you can really taste the difference in the food. Spend a little more at the checkout line and worry a little less in the kitchen.

Next, keep it simple when it comes to the kinds of dishes you're preparing. He suggests a good first dish to try out is shrimp, and it's preferable to buy ones that have already been deveined and shelled. They're versatile and hard to screw up. Just throw them in with olive oil and wait for them to turn pink, which only takes a couple of minutes. Fino is also a fan of red meat because even if it's undercooked slightly, it won't hurt anyone. Chicken, on the other hand, really needs to be cooked

through. If you're short on time but don't want to give your date
salmonella, try my really easy chicken recipe (okay, fine, Anna
taught me this). It involves pounding a chicken with a mallet,
something that incidentally makes you look extra manly:

Place chicken breasts in a large plastic storage bag and seal it.
Pound with a mallet (or rolling pin, small pot, coffee mug, etc.)
   until chicken is flattened to about a quarter of an inch.
Crack one or two eggs onto a plate and beat with a fork.
On another plate sprinkle equal parts flour and grated
   Parmesan cheese.
Dip chicken breasts in egg, then in the flour and cheese
   mixture.
Transfer to a pan coated in oil or butter and cook both sides
   on medium heat until lightly browned.

I like to serve these with a simple salad of romaine lettuce
and grape tomatoes drizzled with olive oil and balsamic vin-
egar. It's almost impossible to undercook the chicken because
it's so thin after you've knocked the daylights out of it.

While pounding the chicken is easy, it doesn't always get ladies
in the mood. Foods like oysters, chocolate, and arugula are said
to turn women on, but I checked it out and the science behind
aphrodisiacs is inconclusive at best. Fino suggests a nice bottle
of wine. It not only increases the romantic atmosphere but it
can mask food that tastes too bland. Remember, reds for heavier
foods like beef, whites for lighter fare like chicken or fish.

Anna also likes to tell me how much she appreciates the
small details. Whether it's picking up a bunch of flowers or
using real place mats and napkins instead of paper towels, these
little touches tend to go a long way. While you're at it, throw
a couple of candles on the table at the last minute and crank

up some Al Green. These things can really take attention away from the food, should it not turn out so great.

When it comes to dessert, Rocky has one piece of advice—one I've heeded since my pecan pie fiasco—stick to the recipe. There's no need to get too fancy and make everything from an expensive cookbook. I recently discovered that my mother's secret family recipe for chocolate chip cookies is the one on the Nestlé Toll House Semi-Sweet Chocolate Morsels bag. Making things from scratch is overrated. Fino said women appreciate that you're making anything at all. Even if all you do is add an egg and some water to a Duncan Hines brownie mix, that in itself can be a real turn-on. Anna likes to tell me that doing the dishes, taking out the trash, and wiping down the table afterward are all really sexy, too. Strange how those activities never get *me* in the mood.

Finally, don't make your date your guinea pig. Only serve dishes you know you can make well. Start off small and work your way up to a three-course dinner. If you've never turned on your stove before, practice with my old standby: breakfast foods. Eggs and pancakes (from a pancake mix) are pretty easy to make and they are usually a big hit—especially if you throw some cheese in the eggs. Then again, if you're cooking a girl breakfast, you probably don't need much help figuring out how to be romantic.

Matchmaking? What Would Rob Do?

The pursuit of love is a dangerous endeavor punctuated by fleeting triumphs and humiliating defeats. Sometimes you have to go all-out to give yourself a chance. For some, this means buying expensive clothes or a flashy car, or doing relentless exercise to achieve an amazing body. For others, this means having someone else do the tough job of scoping out a suitable mate for you. I speak, of course, of matchmakers.

In today's digital age, the challenge of matchmaking seems to have been solved with various Web sites like eHarmony, which claims credit for an average of ninety marriages a day, and Match.com, which boasts fifteen million members. There are also tons of matchmaking Web sites dedicated to specific ethnic groups, such as JDate.com (for Jews), AsianDating.org, and IndianMatchmaking.com.

Regardless of how ubiquitous these Web sites are, online dating is always a little dubious. Even if you are talking to actual prospects and not some pimply teen pranksters, do you really trust them to send you an accurate picture of themselves? This is why I leave matchmaking to the professionals. In the Jewish community, these are known as *shadchens*—Yiddish for matchmakers.

Before I get into what I learned from one of New York's most successful *shadchens*, here's some background on my brief experience with matchmaking. A friend of mine whom we'll call Logan prided herself on finding love connections among all her various friends. The first date Logan arranged for me was with her friend Lara. Lara was "really pretty and so much fun to hang out with" and, best of all, available for a date anytime. Sight unseen, I agreed to go out with her. My older brother, Mike, always told me never to go on a date until you have visual confirmation that the girl you're being set up with is not a dog. My brother is a wise man, and I was a moron for not adhering to this rule. Lara was plain-faced and slightly overweight, and had about as much personality as a toad.

I compounded my first mistake by asking Lara to dinner, which meant I was booking her for the entire evening. This created a lot pressure for things to go well, and of course they didn't. Talking to her was like wading through a vat of day-old oatmeal—it was slow, not particularly pleasant, and terribly bland. She also had some eating issues. We ordered six sushi rolls and she barely touched anything. Not wanting to see good food go to waste, I proceeded to stuff myself silly until I nearly keeled over from nausea. Then I lied about having to wake up early the next day for work, gave her a weak hug, and literally ran back to my house to puke my guts out.

Logan eventually redeemed herself . . . sort of. When a friend of hers from high school moved out to L.A., where I was then living, she didn't set us up on a date, but she did invite us both to a number of parties she threw that year. That friend turned out to be Anna, who was averse to the idea of meeting strange guys. It took me over a year of seeing her at random gatherings to convince her I wasn't some creepy dude you'd meet on a blind date or on the Internet.

So how does a real pro handle matchmaking? I asked Shoshanna Rikon, who bills herself as "New York City's number one matchmaker." She told me her job is a combination of networking and salesmanship, and that it's "almost like selling stocks and bonds." Shoshanna is constantly on the prowl attending events, going to clubs, making appearances at parties, all so she can add people to her list of potential matches for clients. Her biggest asset is her Rolodex. Because she knows a wide range of people with various looks and personality types, she has a lot to choose from when setting people up. She also does a fair amount of arm-twisting. She told me she'll say things like, "You don't understand . . . this is someone you *need* to meet." Sometimes to get a fire going, you need to throw in extra kindling or drench it in gasoline, as the case may be.

Finding a good match for someone has to do with more than just knowing two single people, Shoshanna said. She tries to figure out what her client is looking for in a mate. Is this an older guy looking for a younger woman? Someone who's outgoing, or a quiet and passive person? Are they looking for an artsy type or a sporty type? These are some of the things that dating Web sites do in matching up like profiles, but Shoshanna relies on intuition and experience to make matches happen, and she doesn't stop after the introduction.

Matchmakers also coach. Shoshanna said part of her success comes from telling people how to be good daters. She tells people to avoid coming on too strong—like a guy who tried to write her a song called "My Shoshanna" that went to the tune of "My Sharona." She also recommends choosing a safe dating environment to help the couple get over the initial awkward hump and get them going on the right path. In the case of my horrible date with Lara, she told me I should have met her for coffee or a drink instead of a long, drawn-out dinner. She likes to put people in a relaxed environment where they can talk and get to know each other without making major commitments.

This is ultimately how Logan succeeded as a matchmaker with me. She didn't have some amazing insight about who worked great together, but she's someone who throws great parties that a lot of people like to come to. Perhaps the best way to be a matchmaker is to get a lot of single people together in one room, put out some food and drinks, and then get out of the way. Just remember not to serve sushi.

Singing a Love Song Like Air Supply: What Would Rob Do?

By the time you're at the stage of your relationship where you're thinking about writing or singing a love song to your significant other, things should be going along well. Also by now you've dropped the "L-bomb"—that is, you're saying out loud that word that rhymes with "shove." If you're not sure you're in love, check your schedule. Are you giving up watching football for shopping-mall time and you don't even care because you're too damn happy? Buddy, you've made it, and now it's time to take it to an even higher level. I'm not suggesting you start ring shopping yet, but if you want to buy yourself some extra points for some of the inevitable bumps that lie ahead, consider writing and performing a love ballad.

My career as a love-song composer began at an early age. When I was in elementary school, I was a big fan of hair bands like Def Leppard, Poison, and, of course, Bon Jovi. I wanted to be just like them so I harassed my mother into getting me guitar lessons. My teacher Elliot was a great guy—he had the most perfect Jewfro, putting a pre-baldness Howie Mandel and pre–receding hairline Billy Crystal to shame—with a warm, sincere smile to match.

Bono once famously paraphrased country singer Harlan Howard when he sang that all he needed was "a red guitar, three chords, and the truth." I came away from four years of lessons with a black-and-white electric guitar (Bar Mitzvah present), six chords, and a profound disillusionment about how good a musician I was. Over my years of intense study, I created a self-penned book of songs heavily influenced by Mr. Bon Jovi and his poetic love ballads. While he wrote songs with names like "Livin' on a Prayer," I wrote songs like "Rock for Love" and "Rock Me Always." I was a heartbreaking rock star in the making—never mind the fact that all my songs were just variations of those six chords I knew, or that I didn't have a woman worthy of hearing these heartfelt songs.

My return to earth came during a junior high school "cof-feehouse," where aspiring teen musicians performed in front of a crowd of aspiring teen slackers. It would be my first per-formance, and I was so excited I didn't bother practicing. My song was U2's "Desire." I played a simplified three-chord variation that uses A, E, and D in various strumming pat-terns. I knew the chords, had a passing familiarity with the lyrics, and had even brought along my harmonica, which I'd never tried playing for more than five minutes. As you might have guessed, I stank. At one point, I forgot whether I was supposed to be singing, playing, or blowing on the harmonica and I wound up blowing into the microphone. Adding to my misery, some other guys from my grade got up with their guitars and wound up being decent, playing a whole array of bar chords that I could never master. When my mother had bought me my electric guitar, I told her I'd play it for years. After that performance, I stowed that thing away and haven't opened the case since.

For my twenty-fifth birthday, I decided to give the guitar one more try. I bought myself a Taylor acoustic and signed up for some lessons. I learned a few more tricks and was happy to discover that those six chords I had learned years ago came right back to me. I turned to my old friend Bob Dylan and felt great playing his many simple songs. As for performing, I heeded the lessons of the coffeehouse and played alone in my bedroom with the doors shut.

That all changed when I first met Anna. I think part of the courting process is to show no fear, and hide no flaws. I wanted her to see the musically challenged side of me. It was time to bring back the Rob Sachs power ballad.

Thus was born the song "I Love You, Anna"—a title that would have impressed me as a nine-year-old. Here are some sample lyrics played to a variation of A, E, and D chords faintly reminiscent of U2's "Desire":

> You are my one and only girl.
> There ain't no one else in the world.
> I love you, Anna, Anna, Anna!
> I love you, Anna-na-na-na-na!

It wasn't going to win me a Grammy, but I played it for her on her birthday and it went over well. The bar is always set low on the first song, but I realized that if I wanted to continue to write and sing love songs for her, I'd need to step it up. What I needed was the advice of some love song–writing experts. I first thought back to my hair band heroes, but decided to make a play for the all-time kings of love songs—Air Supply. Not only are these balladeers amazing in how their music pulls at your heartstrings, they also appear to share my philosophy that every love song needs to contain the word "love" in the title. Some of their best hits include "Lost in Love," or "The One That You Love," and of course "Making Love Out of Nothing at All." I'm also going to throw in "Here I Am," where the lyrics, "the one that you love," come immediately after the title.

The geniuses behind Air Supply are two Aussies, Graham Russell and Russell Hitchcock. I know what you're thinking, *"That's so funny that there's a duo where one of them has a first name that's the same as the other's last name."* While it may seem cool, it makes it extremely frustrating when you're interviewing them on the phone and you're confused as to whom you're speaking with. In any case, both Air Suppliers were true gents when they let me in on the creative process of writing a love song.

Russell Hitchcock told me that the most important thing when writing a love song is to approach it with *passion*. "It's all about connecting with what you do and what touches you. . . . If you've got passion, you're halfway there." Sounds easy enough, but the other thing you need is some talent, which can be tough to come up with for most of us. My first hurdle is my voice, which never gets deeper than a high tenor. I'm no Barry White, which is a shame since guys with deep bass voices can get away with anything. If James Earl Jones made a CD called *Darth Vader: Love Songs from the Dark Side*, it would instantly go platinum. I went in the other direction and tried singing in falsetto. Nobody can deny there's a ton of great falsetto love songs out there, from the Bee Gees' "More Than a Woman" to Prince's "Kiss" to Color Me Badd's "I Wanna Sex You Up" (a classic in my book).

Graham Russell let me in on another love song secret. According to some Aussie research institute, the name of which he (rather conveniently) couldn't recall, there's a series of notes or chords that, when put together, elicit a powerful emotional response from listeners. Crazy, right? Or it could explain why women always cry when they watch sappy Hallmark commercials or the final love scene in a movie with those dramatic musical swells. It's like there's something inside everyone that takes hold when we hear this particular succession of notes. I tried searching online for these magic chords, but the best I could find were some links to the song "Magic" by the Cars. These chords must be some Aussie secret passed down from Air Supply to INXS to Ben Lee.

What about lyrics? Surely I could improve on "Anna-na-na-na-na." Russell Graham said he takes a cinematic approach to writing a song. "I create a little mini movie in my mind. I see the characters and I say to myself, well what would they do now? And I let them do it my mind, so I see it in front of me. Once I see the action, if you will, then the sounds just come with it."

A good first step is to think of your love song as a little play unfolding, like John Mellencamp's "Jack and Diane" or Janis Joplin's version of "Me and Bobby McGee." A great love song tells the story of your love. With that in mind, I've begun crafting the lyrics for my next smash hit:

> Even your breath smells better
> Whenever our lips are together
> You could have even eaten cheddar
> But I don't care 'cause I found you!

Now, if you think that sounds like Air Supply's "Even the Nights Are Better," you'd be correct. I mean, come on, didn't I already say they're the greatest love song creators of all time? So if you're in a pinch, tweaking a classic is always a sure bet, or you could always rip off one of those Hallmark commercials.

3.

Dude, Get a Grip!

et's face it: it's not easy being a dude. Sure, we've got some physical advantages, like generally being taller or stronger than the opposite sex. But despite all the progress of modern society, there's always going to be a guy next to you trying to tell the world he can mop the floor with you. It's in our DNA. Men are competitive in almost everything we do, whether it's chasing women, gambling, sports, or even eating.

When you're challenged by another guy, your options are few. You either accept the challenge or run home crying to your mommy. I spent far too many years running home—well, not necessarily crying to Mom (though she is pretty comforting)—but I could never figure out the right angle to gain an advantage. Whether it's figuring out how to bargain for the best deal at an open-air market or losing all my poker chips in ten minutes or struggling behind a sea of other dudes to catch the bartender's eye, I've been there. I've even been to a nude beach, the ultimate place where you have to be secure in your manhood.

Yes, it's true that, as the wise Rod Stewart once said, "Some guys get all the breaks." They have more money, they're better-looking, or they're more physically fit. But if you look at history, self-pity gets old fast. There have always been guys who've defied the odds. For example, Allen Iverson is just over six feet tall, a midget by NBA standards, yet he was a perennial All-Star with one of the highest scoring averages in league history. Or take Gordon Sumner, who was a British schoolteacher before he moved to London where, under his new name, Sting, he came to lead one of the greatest rock bands ever. And let's not forget a young copywriter who sank all his money into a magazine called *Playboy*. Hugh Hefner wasn't born wearing that smoking jacket, but he learned to get real comfortable in it.

Natural talents account for something, but gumption along with a little know-how will propel you past the masses. What follows is some of that know-how, but it's up to you to get 'er done.

Playing Poker: What Would Rob Do?

One of the great things about being a dude is that you don't necessarily have to be a great athlete to be deemed a champion. So if you're the kind of guy who gets winded by walking up a flight of stairs, a safe bet would be to master poker, one of the manlier pastimes available. Poker is the alpha male of dude activities for a number of reasons: one, it's slow enough for you to kick back some beers while playing; two, it's exciting, since there's a potential for great monetary gain or loss; and three, it involves using mind tricks.

I'm a natural cheapskate and was never really gung-ho about poker, but over time I've been cajoled into it by my friends. My brother, Mike, taught me how to play, and made me watch the classic poker movie *Rounders* so I could get a sense of how reading your opponents can lead to big money. Yet real-life poker always seemed to be a letdown. Those hands that I took the time to learn about, like royal straight flushes, never appeared. Then there was the constant shuffling and reshuffling of cards that slows down the pace of the game. Most of the time, you win with two pair or three pair, and that's after mixing things up by putting more wild cards into each round. My biggest disappointment in playing poker is the time commitment. Poker is a game for people who are prepared to sit in the same seat for hours on end. The majority of poker games I've played in have ended not because one person won all the money, but because we all just got bored.

Was I doing something wrong? Poker seemed like a lot more fun on TV, especially when the rounds have commentary from Gabe Kaplan, aka Gabe Kotter from *Welcome Back, Kotter*. For some insider tips on what I could do to improve my poker game, I turned to one of the game's own celebrities, Phil Gordon, a professional poker player whose career winnings are well over $2.5 million. He's also the author of *Poker: The Real Deal* and *Phil Gordon's Little Green Book: Lessons and Teachings in No Limit Texas Hold'em*.

Gordon said there are three ways to size up poker players: their betting patterns, their voluntary tells, and their involuntary tells. Watching betting patterns is simply observing how others play. Do they bluff a lot or do they take no chances? The *voluntary* tell is what the player intentionally says while playing. When I used to play with my friends, I lamely tried to psych them out by saying, "Oooh, you better watch out!" right after checking out my cards. Then there are the *involuntary* tells, actions or mannerisms that your opponents make unconsciously. In the Bond flick *Casino Royale*, the villain Le Chiffre bleeds from his eye and 007 mistakes it for a tell, which in turn costs him a good chunk of the Queen's quid. Hollywood would like you to believe these kinds of tells are the most revealing, but Gordon told me that he only "might change one out every thirty decisions based on an involuntary tell." Plus, if some guy at your poker table starts bleeding from his eye, I hope you'd have the decency to get him some eye drops instead of just raising his bet.

Gordon said the best players keep a sharp eye on the play and keep their emotions in check. Being a good player is all about consistency. The key is to develop routines by study-ing each hand and making a calculated judgment of your odds of winning. Gordon's routine involves going down a mental checklist of everything he knows about what's been played and what he's discerned about the other players before he makes his bet. This method may have you folding a lot, but it also may save you from losing all your money and looking like a complete moron for the rest of the night.

As with any other sport, practice makes perfect. Gordon said the more you play, the more you're going to encounter various scenarios and learn how not to be thrown off your game. I was disheartened to find this out, since I figured gambling would be the one sport where any dude can just throw down a wad of cash and go home lucky. That can happen every now and then, but over time the real players win out through a combination of wits and patience. It might take a while to get to Phil Gordon's level, but let's not forget, you'll be able to enjoy the copious amounts of junk food and beer regardless of how you play. Just remember to use a Wet-Nap before your pick up your cards.

Eating at a Buffet: What Would Rob Do?

I feel very deprived to have grown up twenty-five hundred miles away from Las Vegas. I didn't make my first trip to Sin City until my twenty-second birthday. I was a year late and missed having an epic twenty-first birthday there. I'm also sorry to report that I didn't even go crazy on my twenty-second birthday trip, because I was with my parents (what was I thinking?). The craziest thing that happened on the trip was seeing a Wayne Newton show. I have to say regarding Mr. Newton that it's a particularly cruel thing for a singer to have a hit song (in his case "Danke Schoen") that requires his vocal chords to hit high notes that are virtually impossible to reach after middle age. But Mr. Newton did his best—after all, he *did* start his performance by emerging on stage in a space suit.

Luckily, something worthwhile came out of my experience: discovering the amazing treasure trove of mass cuisine in Vegas. It's true, one of the best meals you'll ever have is at a Las Vegas buffet. Up until that point, the only "all you can eat" experience I had was the salad bar at the Old Country Buffet. Now, having seen the beauty of Vegas buffets, I feel the need to spill some of Old Country's gravy on the floor in homage to the great eateries of Sin City.

I wish I could tell you my first Vegas buffet experience was everything I could ever hope for and more. Unfortunately, on that fateful day when I was handed a tray and a white plate and told to go forth and eat, I blew it. I was too impatient to wait for anything from the carving station, or to survey the entire scene before making my selections. Instead, I rushed to the closest ladle I could reach, shoveled food onto my plate, and started inhaling. Before I knew it, I was full from grub I probably could have whipped together myself from my cupboards at home. When I went back for dessert, I loaded up on two different cakes, which I didn't enjoy but felt compelled to wolf down for bragging rights. I hadn't even started gambling and I already felt cheated, save for experiencing Mr. Newton's space landing.

In hindsight, that wistful promise of "all you can eat" was what did me in. Even though I'd never formally trained to stuff my face with hot dogs Kobayashi style, I had a fantasy that my gut was prepared to handle a sumo-sized meal. Recognizing that I have to be choosy is probably the first and most important lesson of getting the most value out of a Vegas buffet.

To figure out exactly what I should be choosing, I called Craig Taylor, executive chef at Treasure Island's buffet, part of the MGM buffet empire. The first thing to watch out for is what Taylor called "filler foods." These are the fifteen different varieties of pasta and other starchy foods, usually placed in the buffet's front row, where they are extremely easy to access. The casinos want you to fill up your plate with this stuff because it costs them next to nothing to make.

What's more, Taylor confessed that casinos often intentionally make it difficult for you to reach their most expensive foods. They tend to stick the big-ticket items way in the back, underneath those sneeze guards, so you have to really struggle to maneuver the ladles or tongs to get what you want. If you have to bend over and contort your body to get those slippery little shrimp, maybe you'll only make one or two attempts to land them on your plate. The casinos are banking that you'll give up from exhaustion or from the tension created by the line of husky customers behind you waiting for their turn at the ladle. Don't give in to pressure. You paid your money to scoop as much as you want, so if you find some good stuff, scoop until it hurts.

That said, don't go crazy on the first platter of A-list shrimp you see. According to Taylor, start your buffet experience by taking the lay of the land. Then plot out your eating strategy. Don't be afraid to think about your meal as a series of multiple trips to the buffet. As mesmerizing as the orange glow of the heat lamps may be, don't forget about the other areas of the buffet. Taylor told me that the best food at Treasure Island, and also the most expensive, is the stuff they have at the carving station. He admitted that "those ribs aren't cheap."

Taylor's confessions helped reinforce a new buffet tactic I've been employing since my Vegas disaster. I call it "Shortest-Line Grab and Go." Say there's a huge line of people at the salad bar. Head straight to the area with the shortest wait, grab what's free, then be prepared to circle back when the action cools down at the other spots. The trick here is to be moderate in your portions and stay away from the starches.

Also, don't be afraid of odd food combinations, because premium chow such as sirloin and jumbo shrimp brought out of the kitchen piping hot go fast. Some people try to put items on a smaller dish to carry in the same hand as their dinner plate, but this is a dangerous maneuver. You run the risk of dropping everything—and trust me, you don't want to be the guy whose crashing plates bring the whole room to a silent standstill. I'm a big fan of letting all the foods mingle on the plate. Your stomach certainly doesn't care how the food gets there, and you might discover a great new flavor combination, like prime rib and doughnuts.

Lastly, if you're getting too frustrated by the awkward placement of choice foods in the back of the serving tray underneath a cumbersome sneeze guard, do some warm-up exercises while you're waiting in line. Wrist circles, shoulder rolls, and side bends will help limber up your body for the formidable contortions necessary to reach the Holy Grail of buffet items. Also, consider bringing your own ladle with an extra-long handle and a wide basket for optimal scooping. Or make your own by attaching something long, like a rolled up *Playbill* from a Wayne Newton show, to one of their ladles with some duct tape. Practice hard, and you'll beat the house at their own game.

Eating Hot Peppers: What Would Rob Do?

These days, if you're heading out to grab a bite to eat with your buddies, you're just as likely to go for tacos and burritos as you are for a burger and fries. According to the Food Marketing Institute, sales of Mexican food are on the rise, and salsa has eclipsed ketchup as the number one condiment in the United States. As Mexican food becomes more ubiquitous across America, your ability to navigate the cuisine's hotter flavors is increasingly crucial.

This brings us to the topic of hot peppers. I had my first experience with a hot pepper as a hapless gringo in eighth grade. There was a festive dinner at school to celebrate the arrival of our Mexican exchange students. The lunch ladies served special dishes like enchiladas and pinto beans and rice. The tables were decorated with real chili peppers, which were meant simply for ornamentation, not for consumption. But when there's a pack of peppers sitting out in front of a bunch of pimply boys who are just a wee bit overconfident, having sprouted their first chest hairs, you're bound to have a dare.

Having recently overcome an unfortunate bout of voice cracking, I felt compelled to assert my developing manhood. I raised the chili high, lowered it into my mouth and chomped down. It had the crunch of the bell peppers I was used to eating in my mom's dinner salads. There was no immediate pain, so I showed off a little by chewing openly and swizzling the pepper—seeds and all—around in my mouth. Then it hit a few seconds later, a firestorm of throbbing pain engulfing my mouth. I grabbed a glass of water and tried drinking it. That helped a little but not enough, so I stuffed my mouth full of bread, using it like gauze in the hopes that it would soak up the pain. Tears welled up in my eyes, and I rushed outside before my friends could see me cry. In ten minutes, the pain had subsided but the streaks of dried tears on my cheeks gave me away.

Even as an adult I still find myself gun-shy around hot peppers. As I walk through the aisles of gourmet stores, I marvel at the rows of specialty hot sauces with names like Crazy Mother Pucker's and Ass in the Tub Hot Sauce. I imagine the creators of these sauces find sadistic pleasure in inflicting pain on others. In fact, getting back at customers was the impetus behind one of the better-known hot sauces, Dave's Insanity Sauce. The inventor, David Hirschkop, created his devilish concoction as a means of retaliation against drunken college students loitering around his burrito shop in College Park, Maryland. Dave told me that the secret behind his sauces is how he extracts the hottest parts of the hottest peppers.

You may be wondering how to know which peppers are the hottest without tasting them all yourself. For that you need the Scoville Rating System. This system was developed back in 1912 by American chemist Wilbur Scoville to measure the hotness (or piquancy) of hot peppers. The hotness in peppers comes from the chemical compound capsaicin. The more capsaicin a pepper's got, the more your face will feel like it's on fire when you eat it. A pepper's hotness is measured in Scoville Heat Units (SHUs). Green pepper–based Tabasco sauce has an SHU rating of 600 to 800. Step things up to a jalapeño pepper, and the SHU rating is anywhere from 2,500 to 8,000. A habañero pepper is in the 100,000 to 350,000 SHU range. If you're feeling completely suicidal, India's naga jolokia pepper has been tested at over a million SHU.

Even with all that "fire," you're not actually getting burned, said Dave. Capsaicin only stimulates pain receptors. It doesn't actually char your skin. He said the only way you could get hurt is if you have very sensitive skin that could blister after eating a pepper, or if you have respiratory problems and inhale the fumes of really hot peppers cooking. He also cautioned against eating a hot pepper while driving. Assuming you're not navigating your way through rush-hour traffic or operating heavy machinery, here's some advice for taking on those spicy little suckers.

Your first step should be preparation. Not all chili peppers are alike—and what's more, it's possible for peppers from the same plant to have different SHU ratings. While you and your buddy might both be eating habañeros, yours could be a lot hotter than his. The only way to find out, though, is to test it. Dave suggested taking a tiny nibble first to see what you're working with before you dive in. If you're still fearful of what you're getting into, Dave let me in on a secret. Professional hot pepper eaters are known to coat their mouths in vegetable oil before a competition.

Eager to test this out in my own science experiment, I enlisted David Kestenbaum from NPR's science desk. Kestenbaum has both the intelligence (with a PhD in physics from Harvard) to thoughtfully analyze my findings and the naïveté to help me out without asking too many questions. In no time I had him swigging Crisco oil with me, straight from the bottle. I'm not sure whether the Crisco helped us, though I now know swigging vegetable oil induces a nasty gag reflex (fortunately neither of us puked).

With our mouths oil-coated, we were ready to take on the array of peppers I had purchased at Whole Foods. I had everything from the fairly innocuous banana pepper to cayennes, jalapeños, and the dreaded habañero. I also brought pepper "chasers" to counteract the capsaicin attack, which included milk, hot dog buns, water, and a cup of ice. Dave of Dave's Insanity Sauce told me the only certain antidote to hot pepper overload was something cold. I made sure the cup of ice was close by.

Kestenbaum and I began with the banana pepper. After a few chews I noticed a small burn in my mouth, but nothing like what I had experienced back in eighth grade. As my initial trepidation dissipated, my cockiness got the best of me. Timid nibbles turned into big bites while we made our way through the cayenne, the jalapeño, and that nasty orange habañero all without shedding one tear. Had I acquired a taste for hot foods? Then all of a sudden the five-alarm fire was a-blazin'. Forget systematically trying out the various antidotes I had in front of me. I grabbed everything at once, stuffing buns in my mouth and gulping down milk, but nothing worked. The ice may have helped the most, but the pain was overwhelming. I could barely speak. Kestenbaum's vast knowledge of the laws of the universe didn't help him either. His eyes swelled with tears and his voice was reduced to a whimper.

What did I learn? First, if you're ever in a situation where you're eating a hot pepper, it's wise to nibble before chomping, and make sure you have something cold available—ice cubes, slushies, frozen peas, whatever you can find. Second, eat slowly and give the capsaicin some time to work its magic. Finally, find an excuse to leave the scene before the real pain sets in. You probably only have a minute or so to grab some ice and head for a bathroom stall where you can sit and sob in solitude.

Coming Up with a Catchphrase: What Would Rob Do?

Today's society is fast-paced, and attention spans seem to be getting shorter than ever. Politicians have learned how to articulate their key points in short sound bites that lend themselves to being repeated on the cable news channels. Images on TV commercials change every one and a half seconds. Shows like E!'s *The Soup* distill hours of talk shows down to easily digestible clips. We've been taught by the media to attach a quick identifier to a person or a thing and move on. To stand out in this society, you need to be catchy, succinct, and a bit sassy.

What you need is a good catchphrase.

A catchphrase is something that's easy to say and is repeated over and over until it becomes part of the national vernacular. A great catchphrase can live forever. Think about Gary Coleman in *Diff'rent Strokes* asking, "What you talkin' about, Willis?" or *The A-Team*'s Mr. T barking, "I pity the fool!" or *Fantasy Island*'s Tattoo shouting, "De plane, de plane!" These shows have been off the air for years, but their catchphrases endure. Catchphrases don't even need to be real words. Remember the Fonz's "Aaaay!" on *Happy Days*? And who could forget Joey Lawrence's character on *Blossom* responding to everyone with his signature "Whoooah"? The cable network TV Land ranked the top one hundred TV catchphrases of all time. Number one on the list was Ed McMahon's "Here's Johnny!" from *The Tonight Show*.

You don't need to be on a network TV show to have your own personal catchphrase. In high school, I had a friend named Anwar who always used the word "shabby." Of course we'd all heard of the word, but Anwar made it *his* word. It was the key ingredient to his catchphrase, "That's so shabby!" It turned out to be an extremely versatile phrase, as it could mean anything from "That's so cool!" to "That's so pitiful!" to "That's such a poorly made piece of clothing you're wearing." I knew Anwar had achieved complete success when other people in the school began using derivations of shabby in everyday speech. Example: "That's totally *shabbadocious*." It got to the point where Anwar started going by the nickname "Shabwar."

Even kids in other grades who didn't know Anwar knew about his nickname. Shabwar became a legend.

I tried my luck at introducing some catchphrases of my own in high school, but they never got very far. There was a time when the word "salty" was getting a lot of usage, as in "I'm feeling really salty," which meant you were feeling like a loser. I tried to take things to the next level by weaving it into catchphrases like "You're such a salt dog," or "Pass the pepper 'cause someone's all salty." Eventually, I had to set the salt dog free because, well, he was pretty lame.

In my adult life, I haven't been able to find myself the perfect catchphrase, that one cool word combination I can repeat over and over that will make people laugh and high-five me every time. It was time to call an expert. Who could I call? I tried calling Mr. T (seriously), but he was unavailable. So I got in touch with the man who has made a whole career out of one phrase: "Let's get ready to rumble!" His name is Michael Buffer, and he's the proud owner of the nineteenth spot on TV Land's catchphrase list.

If we're judging on money alone, "Let's get ready to rumble!" may be the most successful catchphrase of all time. Buffer's Web site boasts that he's been able to market that one trademarked phrase into more than *$400 million* in combined gross retail revenue from licensing fees. Buffer didn't hit on his signature phrase right away. When he started announcing boxing matches, he tried to psych up the crowd with phrases like "And now man your battle stations!" but they went nowhere. Buffer told me that "Let's get ready to rumble!" is his riffing off the word "rumble," which had long been used as a boxing euphemism, as in the Muhammad Ali–George Foreman 1974 "Rumble in the Jungle." Buffer tinkered around until one day he tossed out "Let's get ready to rumble!" When he saw the crowd's reaction to the phrase, he knew he was on to something. The more he repeated it, the more he became associated with it. After a long process of getting the phrase trademarked, he now has complete control over who gets to use it for commercial purposes.

Buffer has also adapted variations of the phrase, recording "Let's get ready for roundball!" for the NBA, and "Let's get ready to crumble!" for a Kraft cheese commercial. I suggested he try out "Let's get ready to tumble!" for a Maytag dryer commercial. (I'm guessing it didn't work out, since I haven't seen this one on TV.)

How did Buffer do it? Having a large audience to test your material out on always helps. It's great if you can get the microphone at a big public event if you're trying out something new, but if this isn't possible, get in front of any large group to gauge the reaction to your catchphrase. If the response is only ho-hum, ditch it and move on.

Also, try a catchphrase that's a variation on something already in the cultural ethos. The trick is to put your own signature spin on it. Use action phrases and cool slang, the more current the better. Cultural references work too. Check lists of the newest words added to the dictionary and try to weave them into something.

Next, it's important to work on your delivery. Say your catchphrase with some flair, like the way Buffer draws out his L's: "Lllllllets's get ready to *rumbllllle*!" You've also got to be committed to repeating this phrase over and over again to make sure everyone associates it with you. Say it all day long to friends and relatives, or make YouTube videos of yourself using it in public. Your goal is to get it stuck in people's heads so they start repeating it and spreading it too.

Sometimes the hardest part of having a great catchphrase is knowing where to start. Even with a set of fun new words that you think may click, you can get catchphrase-writer's block. Sometimes I'll try to pick a cool word and insert it out of context everywhere I can until something hits that's particularly catchy. Or you can just buy some Mad Libs and toss your new words in there to see if anything good comes out. The key is to use something familiar and brand it into something new.

And if you have kids, keep a notepad handy. It's absolutely true that they say "the darndest things." I've taken to writing down some of my six-year-old nephew's crazy talk. So far all I've got is "I'm going to stick you in the underwear drawer!" Thanks, Oliver! I'm not sure if that has any real chance of catching on. But perhaps I can convince Buffer to approve my using the phrase "Let's get ready to stick you in the underwear drawer!" Now, *that* has some potential.

Underdressed for a Party? What Would Rob Do?

The toughest part of a party night is often just getting out the front door. These days, guys are scrutinized just as much as the ladies for what we wear. The times when getting ready to go out meant throwing on a pair of blue jeans and a white T-shirt are over. This is the era of the metrosexual. Sniffing your clothes to see if they'll hold up one more night doesn't work anymore because "going out" can mean so many different things now. Are you going to a get-together with friends? A corporate party with your spouse? Jacket or no jacket? Jeans or dress pants?

What you wear depends on where you're going. Guys do things last-minute, but if this is an event your significant other has invited you to, it pays to ask what kind of attire the occasion you're attending requires.

There are six levels of dress for events:

- Casual: Wear whatever you want.
- Smart Casual: The dicey middle ground—some places specify no jeans, sneakers, or sweats. Slacks or cords work best here, along with black shoes and a button-down shirt or sweater.
- Business Casual: The clothes you'd wear to work, kind of like smart casual but not as hip.
- Formal: Either coat and no tie, coat with tie, or black tie (wearing a tux).
- White Tie: A super tux with tails is required, but white tie parties are stupid and attended mostly by geriatrics with too much money and time on their hands.
- Costume Parties: A wild card and fairly self-explanatory. Two things you should always remember at a costume party: one, don't wear a mask you can't breathe through, and two, don't dress too trashy because you're going to feel pretty self-conscious on your way there and back.

When you're going out to an event, do yourself a favor and ask ahead about those general formality guidelines regarding jeans, sneakers, tie and jacket, and so on.

Now, I have to mention here that there are some people who dare to disregard these rules completely, one of them being Fabio. Yes, *that* Fabio, the international male supermodel. I spoke with Fabio about how to dress, in the hopes of learning how average guys can break free from rigid dress codes. Fabio takes a much more philosophical approach to getting dressed. "When you're comfortable, you're comfortable," he told me.

Fabio offered a lot of other gems, such as, "If you have a balance of mind, body, and soul, it doesn't matter what you're wearing." He seemed confident in his Zen-like Fabiosophy, but I'm guessing women who invite him to parties are usually interested in seeing him in as few clothes as possible. Here's a little bit of Robosophy: If the hair on your back and shoulders is thick enough to puff out your clothing, it's best to keep that covered up.

There's another inherent flaw in Fabio's theories, says my NPR colleague Karen Grigsby Bates, coauthor of *Basic Black: Home Training for Modern Times*. She says being underdressed is flat-out rude. The real reason you need to dress well is not so much to save you from embarrassment, but to respect the people who invited you to the party you're going to. Party dress codes have little to do with wanting to suck away people's individuality, and more to do with the person planning whatever event you're attending putting a lot of thought into the ambience they want to create. Don't be the guy who turns heads with a wacky Hawaiian shirt and neon blue board shorts (unless of course you're at a luau). I've never been that far off, but I have been the one dude wearing jeans when everyone had on pants, or kicking it in my Adidas while everyone else wore loafers. If you're going to a club or fancy restaurant, your casual attire may prevent you from getting in the door. And even if you do get in, get ready for a night of disapproving glances and snarky comments from other dudes, like, "Hey, way to dress up!" The worst, of course, is being caught without a sports coat. There's really no way to hide that.

It's at this moment of the evening when you have to rely on your primordial instincts—fight or flight. If you're not too far from home, you can go back and change. If you've spent an hour slogging through traffic to get to the party, that may not be an option. I would like to say I've always known what to do beyond sulking in the corner and trying not to be conspicuous, but that would be a lie.

What I do know comes from my brother, Mike, who avoided these situations altogether by always leaving a blue blazer and a tie in the trunk of his car. He learned this through years as a brand manager promoting high-end alcohol, which involved partying at various big-budget events replete with open bars and Swedish models. Tough job, right?

If the valet has already sped off with your car, Mike suggests finding a better-dressed friend at the party and getting him to give up some of his formal attire to help you out. For instance, if he's wearing a coat and tie, borrow the tie. If you don't know anybody at the party, allow me to share Mike's greatest move to save you from embarrassment—ask the wait staff to lend you something formal from their outfits, like a jacket, or if it's a real formal affair, maybe you can score a bowtie. You might have shown up in jeans, flip-flops, and a T-shirt, but adding a cummerbund shows people you at least have a good sense of humor about your thoughtlessness.

Getting Past the Nightclub Bouncer: What Would Rob Do?

As any stud worth his Versace jeans will tell you, before you can be Mr. Macho in a club, you have to get through the door. The vast majority of drinking establishments don't have a velvet rope, meaning you can meet a friend there, grab a beer, and watch the game. That said, a woman trying to look as hot as possible is not putting on makeup to have her face glow in the light of a red neon Budweiser sign hanging in a window. According to Steve Frumin, the founder of Universal Promotions, a high-end promotions company based in Boston, the point of making people stand outside at the velvet rope really has little to do with the fire code. It's a very convenient way for the club to use its patrons as an advertisement directed at anyone passing by. It tells the world that this is an exclusive place for exclusive people.

Frumin said it doesn't matter who your dad is, or if you're a friend of a friend of the barback—because if you're not "on the list," no amount of smooth talking will convince the bouncers and that girl with the clipboard you're a VIP. They're not interested, they've heard it all, and putting up a stink only empowers them to pass you over repeatedly as you wait in line. What the people on line don't know is that all those people on that VIP list aren't particularly important either. They're just a little savvier about their club-going experience.

As Frumin explained, getting on the list isn't always a hard thing to do. It could be as simple as calling a night or two ahead to the club and asking to be on the guest list, or inquiring to find out who's promoting the club that night (many times promoters are independent contractors) and asking them directly. If neither of those tactics works, Frumin said to call the concierge at one of the hip hotels in the area and say, "Hey, I'm in town and I'm actually not staying at the W tonight, but I was wondering if you could help me out with a guest list tonight." Crazy at it sounds, Frumin said this often works. The hotel has endeared itself to a future guest, and you've just saved yourself anywhere from fifteen minutes to an hour and a half (or longer) standing outside in a line.

If you haven't prepared that far in advance, and you're standing out in the cold, and you're clearly not on the list, all is not lost. Frumin stressed it's important not to lose your cool. This can often be challenging, especially if you find yourself boiling over with anger as you watch a parade of European dudes pull up in their Porsches and Beemers filled with grade-A blondes, toss their keys to the valet, give that stupid little chest bump to the bouncer (as if they're old pals), and proceed to walk right into the club.

In case you're wondering what these guys have that you don't, Frumin said it's the obvious: money and women. You may not have enough money for a sports car, but you probably have some cash in your wallet. Try discreetly tipping the bouncers. Frumin told me twenty dollars a head is usually the going rate for cutting the line. Just remember, if you're going to tip, be discreet. Walk up to the bouncer, palm the money in your hand and then shake his. Whipping out your wallet from your back pocket only makes you look like a tool. Bribery is for gentlemen, not jerks.

If you want to be a big-time VIP, go up to the front and request bottle service for the night. This not only gets you and all your friends right in the door, but also gives you the privilege of your own private table with a bottle of top-shelf booze and a bevy of mixers. But this tactic doesn't come cheap. Expect to pay between three hundred and eight hundred dollars per bottle, depending on the club and the liquor.

If you're like me and prefer to pay the rent rather than five hundred dollars for a thirty-dollar bottle of vodka, and if you're certain there's no way you're slapping a twenty in the palm of that steroid freak just to get in this club, there's one other option—bring women. Bringing women to a place where you're looking to meet other women seems counter-intuitive, but how about asking your sister and her friends to accompany you, then kissing them good-bye once you get in the door? Frumin said that for most clubs, the optimal male-to-female ratio on any given night is three women for every dude. If you show up to a club with four buddies, you should be asking yourself, where are those fifteen girls you've brought to accompany you? It should go without saying that if you're with a bunch of guys, break up into smaller groups so you all have a better chance of getting in.

Frumin's last piece of advice requires a bit of chutzpah. He said to scope out the line and pick out some women who are standing there (yes, club lines do contain women). Pretend you're the promoter and take them up to the front. Now you've got a nice group to get you in. Does this work? Frumin told me it does, and has the added bonus of introducing you to a bunch of ladies whom you've just rescued from the line. Not only is it a great opener, but it's also a lot cheaper than buying them drinks, which itself can be a whole other indignity.

Ordering a Macho Drink: What Would Rob Do?

Getting a drink seems simple, except when you're at a crowded club or bar where you're competing against fifty other dudes for the bartender's attention. I've been to some bars in L.A. that were so mobbed, I could have bodysurfed to get to the counter. I've waited upwards of half an hour to get one lousy drink. While I've tried out some techniques to cut down on the wait time, I wanted to run them by a true connoisseur of drinking, Frank Kelly Rich. He is the man behind the not-so-subtly titled *Modern Drunkard Magazine*.

Rich said, first, establish bartender eye contact so he or she can put you in their mental queue of people who need a drink. The best way to get that eye contact is to wave the green flag—a twenty-dollar bill—because that says, "Hey, I'm ready to order, I'm ready to pay, and I'm not messing around." You should also be whittling some space for yourself at the bar. The best way I've found to do this is to start off perpendicular to the bar and stretch as far as you can just to get a fingertip on the counter. Any real estate you can physically touch, you own. Once you've got a finger, keep wiggling, and wedge in your elbow until you get a forearm resting nicely on the bar. Before you know it you'll be able to swing your hips around to be completely parallel to the bar. Don't be discouraged if it takes a while to get the bartender's attention. Waiting for a drink offers a great opportunity to meet women as you can bond over your shared frustrations of being ignored.

Once you finally have the bartender's attention, the question is: what do you order? Your manliness is on the line, and whether you realize it or not, women will take note of what you order. If the guy next to you orders a Jack Daniel's on the rocks (eighty proof), don't be afraid to order a Wild Turkey 101 straight-up. If you freeze up, the easiest thing to do is follow George Thorogood's advice: one bourbon, one scotch, and one beer, in that order. Tequila is also an acceptable manly drink. For a good measurement of how brawny your drink is, try the wince test. If you offer a sip to a woman and she winces, you're on the right track. After you swig your fiery tonic, it's not a bad idea to throw in an exclamation like "Mmm . . . dang!" or to pound your chest a few times . . . or not.

If hard alcohol is not your flavor, beer is always a safe bet, though women might read into that order too. If you ask for a light beer (*Why is he counting calories?*) or get a fancy import (*Who's this beer snob?*), you could be in trouble. You could get a throwback beer like Pabst Blue Ribbon, but that can actually go either way. You could be Mr. Cool Retro, or you could be Mr. I'm Trying Too Hard. When ordering beer, I try to go local. Figure out what beer is made in town or in close proximity to wherever you are. It makes you seem like you've got some hometown pride, or that you appreciate the locals. And isn't that the point, to show the local ladies how much you value what they have to offer?

Drinks you should stay away from include anything that comes with an umbrella or is made with maraschino cherries, whipped cream, or chocolate. Also avoid wine. Don't get me wrong. I love drinking it at home, or with dinner at a nice restaurant, but it's an *absolute no-no* at a bar. Ordering a glass of wine is pretentious and lame, akin to wearing an ascot and speaking in a faux British accent. As Frank Kelly Rich pointed out to me, the big problem with ordering wine isn't its inferior alcohol content (in fact, it carries more than double the alcohol of most beer), but the wine glass itself. Those delicate stems, and the sniffing, sipping, and slurping routine may be fine at a Napa vineyard or in a swanky wine bar, but holding a glass of wine at a club makes you look like a tool.

However, if you are still compelled to down some vino, at least order it in something other than a wine glass. Ask for it in a pint glass or a mug—or better yet, see if they have a Viking drinking horn. It doesn't matter what it is, as long as you don't get caught pointing your pinky up in the air while sipping from a dainty little champagne flute. The stemmed glass ban also rules out martinis—shaken, stirred, whatever—because you're not James Bond, even if you claim to have a Walther PPK in your pocket.

Once you get your drink, tip big on the first round. If you want to get noticed quickly the rest of the night, throw in a fiver for a couple beers. You can taper it back after that. Now, if the bar is so packed that it takes you twenty minutes just to order one drink, order a reserve libation while you've got the bartender's attention, preferably a bottled beer. Maneuvering around without the use of your hands does take some getting used to, but there is an upside to this. Should you happen to bump into that friendly lady you saw while waiting for the bartender, you already have a drink to offer her.

Playing Pickup Basketball: What Would Rob Do?

Growing up, I played basketball nearly every day. My neighborhood buddy Vincent and I would shoot one-on-one for hours after school and on the weekends on the hoop that stood on my parents' driveway. That court's life met an untimely demise when my brother decided one night to do a 360-degree stuntman-style doughnut spin into the garage with his car. He almost succeeded, but on the very end of the rotation he nailed the family basketball pole head-on. That pole didn't fall over on impact, but it was fatally injured. The final collapse came a few days later when I was taking shots on the sagging rim. After one particularly hard bank shot, the whole thing gave way and came crashing down about two inches from my face.

Without a hoop at home, I was forced to play at the local park. When I first started going, I would shoot around with some buddies I had called ahead to come meet me at the court. From time to time other people would challenge us to a game of four-on-four. It was all friendly enough until one day I showed up alone and the courts were more crowded than ever.

That's when I learned the code of the pickup game. To my relief, getting into a pickup didn't necessarily require any display of skill. It had more to do with persistence. Usually there's a team of five players waiting to play after the current game finishes. If the person who has organized the players for the next game is short a man, getting in can be as simple as asking if they need one more. When I lived in Santa Monica, there was a guy named Jimmy who hung around the courts all the time. Jimmy was in his midforties and made about one in every thirty shots he took, but he was constantly playing. It's not that people were excited to have Jimmy on their team, but whenever you needed an extra player, Jimmy was always there to jump in.

But just because you helped fill a team's roster, don't think you can get away with completely stinking it up on the court. Your teammates won't pass you the ball if they see you're terrible. The biggest street-ball sins include being a gunner who tosses up three-point shots you don't make, and playing lousy defense. Since most pickup games are played man-to-man, if the guy you're defending is scoring at will, your teammates won't be too pleased.

There's also the issue of setting picks. By their nature, pickup teams never have set plays, but that doesn't mean that you can just stand around and wait for someone to pass to you when you're on offense. A good street baller is constantly trying to get open or get his teammates open. Doing so involves the art of setting picks, or running up to someone else's defender and standing in their way so your teammate can get an open look at a jump shot or layup. Not only do you have to be running around standing in front of people, you have to be aware of when people are trying to do this for you.

The other important thing is to get out of the way. When your teammate has the ball, find the spot on the court where nobody else is standing, or keep moving around. This is easier said than done. I know I'm really stinking things up when every other guy is shouting at me to "run through"—in other words, move my butt to the other side of the court. When all else fails, I stand underneath the basket. In organized basketball, standing there would be a three-second violation for camping out and waiting for a rebound, but in pickup ball, this rule is ignored. If you stink at shooting, grabbing rebounds off your teammates' missed shots will make you a valuable asset to the team.

My work at NPR moved me from the palm tree–lined courts of L.A. to the stinky ginkgo tree–lined courts of D.C. It was a new locale for me, and I needed to know if there were any codes of the court that I was overlooking. I called Chris Ballard, a writer for *Sports Illustrated* and author of a book called *Hoops Nation*, which detailed his experiences touring the country playing on all types of courts. Ballard told me the one requirement in any pickup game is to hustle. If you're running up and down the court and trying to involve yourself in both offense and defense, chances are you're going to help out. There's always going to be at least a few out-of-shape guys playing, and if you're zipping around a lot, you'll create a lot of opportunities for easy baskets for either yourself or your teammates.

Being well conditioned to endure constant hustling up and down the court will allow you to get by in any game, but it won't make you a superstar. Having good basketball fundamentals will help out in any situation, so dust off your skills from junior high gym class. If you don't have a strong background in hoops, there are a couple of basic techniques you can work on. Try making your layups more than 75 percent of the time and practice throwing good tight passes to other players. These two skills alone will make you a better teammate offensively.

Apart from the layup, I think the best thing to do is develop a signature shot. Pick one spot on the court and figure out how to make the basket from there a high percentage of the time. It doesn't matter whether it's a hook shot from the left side or a fadeaway jumper from beyond the three-point arc. If you can add some flair to that signature shot, that's a bonus. I used to practice this one amazing shot against Vincent where I'd hurl the ball from the corner of the court into the basket as I fell into my mother's rhododendron patch. I had to stop this when she took the landscape repair costs out of my allowance, but I'll never forget the disbelief in Vincent's face every time I sank one of those impossible shots.

Once you've mastered your basic and signature shots, and built up some endurance to run up and down the court, you can add style to your game. Alley-oops, dribbling through your opponent's legs, and no-look passes make the game more fun—if you can do them right. There's no quicker way to lose the respect of your teammates than hot-dogging it and messing things up. So maybe try some less complex stylistic moves to start. Like a sweet crossover dribble or a great pump fake before you shoot.

When joining a pickup game, don't be surprised if people play mind games with you. Trash-talking is a big part of the street-balling game. I was never that into it, because it can sometimes lead to fighting. When I get trash-talked, I ignore what they're saying, or give them a big smile. When I play with my friends, though, and have no fear of an all-out brawl, I'll do about anything to throw them off. I've been known to start singing one of those annoying Mariah Carey songs with the really high notes whenever someone's about to shoot. Vincent's personal favorite from elementary school was when I would lift my shirt and smack my stomach right as he was releasing the ball, but you probably don't want to try that move out on strangers.

Chris Ballard's last piece of street-ball advice was to use being an unknown entity to your advantage. Deception is often a big part of winning. You expect the six-foot-six guy with bulging biceps to dominate inside the paint, but look out for that short dude with the glasses and the sneaky outside jumper. Some of Ballard's most successful outings on the court have come when he brought along a female teammate who knew her stuff. I used the art of deception myself whenever I played in Santa Monica. I'd wear Bermuda shorts instead of those mesh basketball shorts and a random thrift store T-shirt instead of a tank top so the good players would think I was out of my element. My plan was to set low expectations and then surprise them with my amazing skills. In your face, buddy! The other great benefit to dressing down is that nobody seems to mind too much should you happen to be having an off day; at that point you can easily slink off the court and slowly fade back into the crowd.

Naked in Public? What Would Rob Do?

It was on a trip to the Bahamas with my parents that I was first introduced to European tourists and the wonders of topless sunbathers. This happened before I hit puberty, so I got away with freely ogling the tanning tatas until my mother scooped me away. When I got older, I had to sneak furtive glances from underneath a baseball cap or behind my Miami Vice–style sunglasses with tinted lenses. As for actually going buff myself, I never had the guts to go bare, as I had a deep fear of, shall we say, getting too excited.

The pinnacle of my topless beach experience couldn't have come at a better time. I was eighteen and spending a summer studying Spanish in Alicante, Spain. It was a complete immersion program, and the course work was grueling. I was learning a year's worth of Spanish in three weeks. Most days after class I took a short bus trip from the university down to the beach, which like all Spanish beaches is top optional. The sands were packed, and I was in heaven . . . at first. On any given day there were at least fifteen topless women to fix my gaze on, but as my time in Alicante wore on, the thrill started to dissipate. I was becoming spoiled. By the end of the summer, I could sit across from a topless sunbather and read a magazine instead of admiring the view. Never had I imagined my libido would allow me to be "mature" about all of this.

Many years later, my soon-to-be wife, Anna, and I were vacationing on the island of Mykonos in Greece. Mykonos is known as a party haven and is filled with many beautiful clothing-optional beaches. Intrigued, we set off on our rented moped and found a spot aptly named "Super Paradise." It was the end of the tourist season, but we still saw a few people in the buff. Unfortunately, the female-to-male ratio was poor, and the few women I did spy had some sagging issues. But of course, there was no need for my eyes to wander since I was with Anna, right?

We found a secluded corner of the beach and tried out au naturel sunbathing until we spotted a sleazy dude with a camera. The whole experience wound up being more creepy than exhilarating. My dream of gallivanting around playing coed naked beach badminton was never to be realized. What I thought would be liberating ended up making me feel afraid to move, trapped on my small patch of sand.

Was my experience in Greece atypical? What is the nudist scene like here in the United States? To find out, I enlisted the help of Erich Schuttauf, the executive director of the American Association for Nude Recreation (AANR). The AANR boasts over two hundred fifty nude recreation facilities in North America, with revenues topping $400 million annually. Schuttauf said people who visit these facilities participate in a whole range of activities including volleyball, golf, and tennis, all while completely in the buff. He didn't mention any nude kickboxing, which I'm thinking is a good thing.

As for my biggest fear, that of being aroused, Schuttauf told me it rarely happens because that's simply not the kind of environment they're creating. A lot of these facilities are actually family friendly, so it's much more about people frolicking around naked than getting it on in the grotto. Should you have a rising threat from your libido, Schuttauf said there are any number of ways to tamp things down. He said a quick jump in a cold shower or swimming pool usually suppresses any urges. Also, most of the time you will have something to hide under, as most nudists, or naturists (as some prefer to call themselves), carry around a towel—not for covering up but more for wiping down. In general, people rarely violate the code of nudist ethics at these facilities. Where you have to be more cautious, Schuttauf warned, is at clothing-optional beaches, because they attract more curiosity seekers who aren't familiar with nudist etiquette.

Schuttauf said the best approach to a code violator is to be upfront and forthright about the rules of nude beaches in a way that's least confrontational. The AANR has something called a "beach etiquette" card, which it distributes to its members to give away should a situation occur. The card includes "gentle reminders" ranging from codes on how to be respectful to strict policies about absolutely no sexual activity. It also includes information on who to call to report a violation. If you're someone who has been given one of these cards, take it seriously. Like many misunderstood groups, naturists are quick to defend each other when one of their own is threatened. Ogle one nude sunbather, and you may have to face the wrath of a gang of burly buff men giving you a firsthand lesson in proper etiquette. You'd better pray they remember to bring their wipe-down towels. Sadly, no knickerless knights showed up to save Anna and me at the beach in Greece.

Schuttauf emphasized that the thing he loves most about nude recreation is how liberating it is. He said the more you try out being nude, the more you realize any activity can be that much better when done in the buff, from reading a book to washing your dog (yes, he actually said that)—there are tons of activities you can enjoy in your birthday suit.

Amazingly, nudist retreats even have a business application. Schuttauf told me that all AANR board meetings are conducted in the nude because it's a lot more fun talking business when you're in a relaxed and free environment. He mentioned that in places like Finland, it's common for men to discuss business while naked in a sauna. I can't say I'm eager for one of these work retreats at NPR. An old joke in the office is to quip, "That guy's got a face for radio." I don't think we want to verify that our bodies are made for radio as well.

Flea Markets: What Would Rob Do?

Sometimes your greatest adventures can happen right around the corner from your house. I have fond memories of looking at antiques at local flea markets with my mother when I was growing up. She collected funny things like vintage cookie cutters or strange kitchen tools. To this day, there's a nineteenth-century ice cream scoop hanging up on her kitchen wall.

I never thought much of these knickknacks until I got hooked on PBS's popular program *Antiques Roadshow*. To find out if my mother's collection might be worth something, I called Gordon S. Converse, an antique-clock dealer from Philadelphia and frequent appraiser on the program. He said they interview about five hundred people to find those two or three people worth filming for the show. That means only around one half of one percent has items that are worth anything. My mother has a good eye for stuff, but I don't think she has any gold mines in her kitchen.

Converse added that if you really want to get a great bargain, you have to do your research. On *Roadshow*, they make a point of showing people how to distinguish between a valuable object and a fake, and how to pay special attention to the "patina" of the items. The value of an object is far more complex than figuring out whether something is really old. It also has to do with knowing the market for an item and knowing the difference between a rare find and a more commonplace item. "If I go to a flea market and buy something," Converse said, "it's probably because I've read [a] book [about that item]." If there's a book called *The Definitive Guide of Antiquated Kitchen Tools That May or May Not Have Any Value*, that's what I'm getting Mom for her birthday.

Even after doing all the research, there's no guarantee that a trip to the flea market will yield something of value, but these outings can still be enjoyable if you like to negotiate for sport. Apart from used-car dealerships and some electronics boutiques, there are fewer and fewer places in America where you can bargain for goods. At flea markets, everything is negotiable.

I've learned that a morning of haggling with merchants can, if done properly, be a fun activity in and of itself.

On family vacations, while my father did his best to steer us clear of some of the more egregious tourist traps, we would inevitably run into a trinket or tchotchke market where locals would be peddling cheaply made mementos. This is how I learned to bargain.

My father always stuck to a few simple rules:

1. Set a firm price in your head for what you think the item is worth.
2. When you're tossing out a price, start low so you can work back up to the price in your head.
3. Be prepared to walk away.

Walking away is a move that both my parents loved to pull. We had people literally chasing us down the streets worried they would lose a deal: "My friend, my friend, please . . ." My mom's crowning bargaining achievement was a beautiful hand-made alabaster pot that she got on a trip to Egypt for about one-fifth of the asking price. To this day it remains prominently displayed in my parents' living room—less as a piece of art (a cleaning lady chipped it a few years back) and more as a testament to Mom's negotiating skills.

I heard about another tactic (on NPR, of course), which is to name your price, take out your money, and literally put it in the seller's hand. Now you're playing hardball. Mentally, this messes with a merchant's head, because if he doesn't want to do the deal, he has to give the money in his hand back to you. I've tried this one out and it works.

One of the biggest swap meets in the country is the Rose Bowl Flea Market in Pasadena, California. It occurs the second

Sunday of every month and attracts an astounding twenty-five hundred vendors. It takes hours to see all the stuff there, and trust me, most of it is junk. The truth is, most of the truly valuable stuff is being sold in brick–and-mortar businesses like fine antiques shops. That said, with twenty-five hundred vendors, there are bound to be some undervalued goods. I once bought a few 1980s Polo knit shirts there, which I then resold to an upscale vintage shop in Santa Monica. My net profit was about eight bucks, which was only slightly more than the price of gas to drive out to Pasadena and back, but I still considered it a success.

One of my greatest all-time flea market finds was an authentic 1980 Philadelphia Phillies World Series Championship T-shirt. I wore that thing down to its threads. I've also had my share of not-so-great finds. Anna and I once paid thirty dollars for an oil painting because it had a Jewish theme. We felt it was our duty to "rescue" it and give it a home. That thing never made it onto the wall, and after a few months, it was quietly removed from our apartment. I also bought a great green plastic lamp for nine dollars, which I thought was a steal. That too disappeared under mysterious circumstances, which Anna refuses to discuss.

If I've learned anything from these flea market experiences, it's that the people who make money finding undervalued antiques are usually antiques dealers and expert appraisers. If you're a casual shopper, as I am, it's more worthwhile to buy stuff that you like on sight or have a sentimental attachment to. And remember that one man's treasure might be his wife's trash. Be sure to let your significant other know how much these sentimental items mean to you so they don't end up back on a table at another flea market.

4.

You Have Only Yourself To Blame

This chapter is devoted to conquering the goblins that plague us from within, those little tests our bodies throw at us to remind ourselves to be humble. It doesn't matter how much money you make, how high your cheekbones are, or how hot your girlfriend is—treat your body poorly and it might give you a nasty zit right between the eyes or a spare tire in your gut.

As it turns out, zits are the result of a confluence of complex chemical reactions taking place right underneath the skin. I asked the good people of *Men's Health* magazine to help me unlock epidermal science. The antidote to these nasty abominations may already be in your bathroom.

Speaking of unwanted chemical reactions, have you wondered what's behind the flagrant foulness of flatulence? After exploring the foods that make you toot, I talked to an out-of-the-box inventor who has found a way to take the bite out of your trouser barks. Further expounding on my admittedly juvenile fascination with all things pertaining to the colon, I share a few helpful hints on the best way to find a bathroom when out in public, which naturally leads into another one of life's most dreaded predicaments, what to do should you clog the bathroom toilet.

I also have tips for dealing with how our bodies try to sabotage us in our sleep. There's hope for anyone who snores like a deranged yeti, or gnashes away at their teeth like a rabid beaver. I turned to two experts who have studied the inner workings of the body for solutions. The first is an MD who explained the connections between a soft palate and a loud snore. The other is a hypnotist who revealed that a persuasive voice in a relaxed environment will help you to stop biting your nails, cease grinding your teeth in your sleep, and quit your three-pack-a-day smoking habit.

While we're on the topic of hypnotists and mind games, I talked to an expert who said he can make you smarter. . . . Well, he *can* help boost your memory. You'll learn how to remember the names of all those people you meet whose names you forget two seconds later.

Having someone fix your head is great, but other bad habits require the persistence of the people around you to help you change your ways. I found out from a clutter expert that it often takes the objective voice of a friend or a spouse to help you let go of the junk that is taking over your life. And speaking of voices, I also explore some of the secrets behind keeping your voice in prime shape. I learned from a professional opera singer how she keeps her vocal cords well tuned and ready for each performance.

Next, I delve into the best ways to get into better shape by talking to one of the most influential trainers in the country. Despite what the diet and health club industries have said, he told me that getting fit and building real strength require getting off the treadmill to pump some iron.

Finally, I face the fear we feel every time we sit down in front of that strange man with the sharp scissors, the barber. How do you best cope with getting a bad haircut? And how do you maintain those flowing locks on your own? For answers on getting good hair, I went to the stylist for *American Idol*, also known as the "Hollywood Hair Guy." He sometimes refers to himself as a "hair ho," but we don't need to get into that.

Our bodies have a way of keeping us from getting too vain and too confident, and remind us in myriad ways that yes, we are all mere mortals. By understanding some basic biology, psychology, and modern plumbing, you'll be better prepared the next time you get attacked from within.

Conquering Bad Habits: What Would Rob Do?

Everyone has bad habits, from nail biting to talking with your mouth full to leaving the toilet seat up in the bathroom. I'm guilty of all these things in some shape or form. Bad habits are hard to break because we often do them unconsciously. When I was in Little League, I somehow developed the habit of throwing my bat after I got a base hit. I was told repeatedly not to throw that Louisville Slugger, but it was like asking a lion to check if his paws were clean before he pursued an antelope.

During a night game on the baseball field at McKinley Elementary, I slammed a line drive out to right field. I knew that if I ran I would get extra bases, since nobody knew much about fielding at that age. In my zeal, I burst out of the box expecting to hear cheers. Instead, I heard screams. I had nailed some poor girl sitting by the third-base line on her arm. It turned out to be a minor bruise, but seeing those tears from that innocent lass (along with the disapproving stares from the parents in the stands) cured me of that bad habit for good. I still feel awful about that one.

None of my adult bad habits cause bodily harm to unsuspecting bystanders, but I still have one I desperately want to kick. I grind my teeth in my sleep. It began when I was learning how to drive a stick shift on my brand-new car. Every time I ground the gears, my teeth would follow. It was agony thinking about how much a new clutch was going to cost me.

Well, one clutch and a few thousand dollars later, I'm proud to report that I've successfully learned how to drive my own car. However, the teeth grinding stayed along for the ride.

I asked my friend and long-suffering teeth grinder Mitch for help. He said hypnosis cured him completely. I couldn't believe it! Had somebody really swung a watch in front of his face and convinced him to stop gnashing away? Mitch said yes, though it wasn't quite like that. To test out Mitch's theory, I found a Web site called INeedMotivation.com, which looked like a perfect match for my problem. Yes, I definitely needed motivation. "I Need Motivation" is the name of an audio program started by Frederic Premji, who prefers to describe his program as "relaxation therapy" instead of hypnosis.

Premji told me his technique is to use "logic and motivation induced within a relaxing environment." In essence, he's making a persuasive argument in a relaxed state to get people to eliminate habits such as smoking, gambling, and teeth grinding. For instance, his nail-biting CD says that "you will keep your fingers far away from your mouth, the farther the better." Premji insists that these messages sink into our subconsciousness when presented in the right environment and can make all the difference in changing people's actions.

I sat down in a comfortable chair, took a deep breath, and listened to some of the samples he has online. I didn't make it past the first ten seconds. As someone who prides himself on his vast music collection, I immediately objected to his choice of putting a New Age sound track in the background. Instead of feeling soothed, I felt angered by a tune that was trying hard to be "emotionally inspiring." To me, Yanni and his New Age brethren are about as inspiring as a cat poster that says "Hang In There!"

Cheesy music aside, hypnosis isn't for everybody. Some people are too skeptical or consider themselves too intelligent to listen to a stranger's suggestions. Conversely, people with an IQ under 70 are likewise often cited as being impossible to hypnotize. What to do, then, if hypnosis doesn't work? Sometimes there's no shortcut or substitute for good old-fashioned medical advice. To rid myself of teeth grinding, I consulted my dentist, who gave me a mouth guard. This is a very expensive piece of hardened plastic that's taken from a mold of your mouth and prevents your teeth from grinding together. It also makes you sound like a total dweeb when you try to talk. And once you put it on, say goodnight to romance. There are few things in life less sexy than kissing your wife with a big piece of hard plastic shoved in your pie hole.

Now that I think about it, maybe I need to motivate myself and give that New Age stuff a second chance. I wonder if Premji would be up for making me a recording on how to get over that one.

Need a Public Restroom? What Would Rob Do?

It can happen at any moment. One minute you're out walking, and the next—*shazam!*—code-red potty alert. Finding a suitable place to relieve yourself can be tricky these days, especially with so many businesses run by "anti-bladdites" who hang those "Restrooms for Customers Only" signs everywhere you look. As a frequent traveler and avid city explorer, I've been in this situation many times—crouching over, squeezing my crotch, sprinting through busy streets fantasizing about

Depends diapers. What I've found is that relief can be achieved only with a clear head and a sound game plan.

First, assess your threat level. Can you last a half hour, or ten minutes, or is this an "I need to go immediately" scenario? Once you gauge how much time you have until disaster strikes, you can estimate how widely you should expand your search for a lavatory. Next, run through your assets. Do you have a smartphone with Internet access? Do you have money or valuable goods that can be used as barter? And what are you wearing? Are you dressed inconspicuously so you can zip in and out of a variety of places without being noticed? It's also worth estimating how fast you can run in your current outfit, and how long it will take you to get unzipped once you reach the potty. Taking this thorough inventory is essential in making your next decision.

Let's go through the first of these assets. If you have an iPhone, a BlackBerry, or some other device with Internet access, you're in luck, because there are a number of Web sites devoted to helping you figure out where to pee. Australia even has a National Toilet Map run by the government (www.toiletmap.gov.au). Unfortunately, U.S. tax dollars aren't put to such good use, but there are private toilet locator sites like SitorSquat.com and TheBathroomDiaries.com. The latter site was created by Mary Ann Racin. It claims to be one of the largest databases of public restrooms, with reviews of over nine thousand locations. Her site tells people where they can find public bathrooms and rates restrooms on everything from cleanliness to handicap accessibility. Another unique feature of the site lets visitors in on where they can find those incredible bathrooms that are worth holding out for, what I call "urination destinations." The Bathroom Diaries gives these lavatories the "Golden Plunger Award." Recipients of the Golden Plunger include a bathroom in Hong Kong that's made completely of gold. Here's a description from the Web site:

> The toilet bowls, wash basins, toilet brushes, toilet paper holders, mirror frames, wall-mounted chandeliers and even wall tiles and doors are all made of solid gold. Embedded in the floor at the entrance are gold bars and studding the ceiling are 6,200 diamonds, rubies, sapphires and pearls. The store's owner was inspired by Vladimir Lenin's vision of gold toilets for the masses.

Though I haven't visited any Golden Plunger Award recipients, I have plenty of experiences with some of the *worst* bathrooms around. My own "Dungy Plunger Award" goes to a "rest area" I discovered while visiting Olduvai Gorge in Tanzania back in the late '90s. It's famous for being the site of one of the earliest human fossils ever discovered. Perhaps the small museum attached to the site was built around the same time that fossil became embedded in the soil, since the men's "restroom" consisted of a freestanding wall about ten yards away from the main building. Behind the wall was an open sloping trench where a golden stream simply flowed down to a hole in the ground. I didn't see what accommodations they had for women, but I'm hoping they at least had four walls.

If you don't have any fancy doodads that will help you locate a Golden Plunger bathroom, you're going to have to use your wits and hunt down the places that are most likely to have public restrooms. These are hotels and restaurants. I always hit big hotels first because the bathrooms are usually the most sanitary. Also, the hazard with going into a restaurant is that you'll have to pretend that you're planning to eat there, or you'll have to pull the "I'm just joining my party in the back" move before discreetly ducking into the restroom. At hotels, you don't need to pretend you're a guest. The lobby is always filled with people coming and going. If you don't immediately spot a restroom, look for signs that point to the ballroom or conference rooms, since the restrooms are usually around there.

If a hotel isn't nearby, choose a restaurant that you're dressed appropriately for and ignore those "Restroom for Customers only" signs. Once you're inside, simply wander through the restaurant without talking to anyone and try to find the can yourself. You'd be surprised how many times you'll get away with this without being questioned. Meandering through a coffee shop is tougher, since often you have to ask for a restroom key. In this case, you might feel obliged to buy a pastry or something small, but remember to pick it up on your way out (it's considered poor etiquette to eat a jelly doughnut at a urinal). If you can't find a restaurant or hotel, another option is to look for government buildings such as libraries, police or fire stations, or DMV buildings—though they might make you take a number before you get to use the potty.

Now, if your threat level is such that you can't hold out for a public location, you have to switch to desperation mode. You can burst into any open storefront and give them the universal sign—the crotch grab—signaling that there's going to be an accident if you don't act fast. Hopefully, they'll just usher you straight back to the employees-only toilet, but if they don't, begging or crying is a lot less shameful than wetting your pants.

The last resort (and I mean *really* last) is public urination, which almost everyone has done at some point. And yes, it's illegal in most places. In New York City a ticket will set you back anywhere from fifty-five to seventy-five dollars. This is where having a buddy helps, since he can be on the lookout for law enforcement. If possible, try to find a shrub, though this can be tricky in a city. I look for the plantings in front of a brownstone, which are often dense enough to offer adequate concealment. If that's not an option, head down an alley. There you're likely to find a big object like a Dumpster that will offer you some coverage. I try to aim away from the Dumpster so I don't get any splashback, and I always fire downhill. I don't want to finish peeing only to have it trail after me. One other thing you can do to divert attention is not to look down while doing the deed. It's amazing how people passing by will look at whatever *you're* looking at, so in this instance keep your gaze on the third or fourth floor of the building in front of you, and with luck they won't notice you hosing down the asphalt.

If you happen to be out with a lady friend and she needs to relieve herself, public urination becomes a much more dangerous undertaking. You will need to find double the shrub concealment, because she will likely take longer than you would. When you're on pee lookout, you're also in charge of running interference. So if somebody is getting too close, you should do whatever it takes to cause a distraction to give your lady friend those precious extra seconds. Ask that person for directions, or a recommendation for a restaurant with a nice restroom. Remember, your friend's dignity is at stake here. If you screw up watching out for a woman while she's peeing in public, you're going to be in deep doo-doo.

Big Fat Zits: What Would Rob Do?

My first big outbreak of zits happened right before my bar mitzvah. This Jewish rite of passage into manhood involved chanting Hebrew in front of all my friends and family, not to mention any other member of the Beth Sholom Congregation who happened to show up for Sabbath prayers. I'm guessing God wasn't satisfied with giving me just one test that day.

When I woke up that morning, I looked into the mirror and found a trail of little white bumps running down the side of my nose like a rogue mountain range. I ran to my mother almost in tears (technically, I wasn't a man until after the ceremony) and showed her my snowcapped peaks of shame.

She took me by the hand and walked me down the hall to her bathroom. She opened the medicine cabinet and took out a pink bag that I had never seen before. When she unclipped the top, she revealed a cosmetics wonderland—concealer, blush, lipstick, and little cases of eye makeup like I'd seen in commercials. I was nervous because makeup was only for women, Boy George, and David Bowie, but I stood still as my mother dabbed my face with cover-up. And then, *presto!* Those gnarly crags were reduced to barely visible bunny hills. Later on, some artful airbrushing by the photographer almost completely erased the outbreak, except from my memory.

Since that day, the makeup drawer has been my friend. Aware of the implications around sexuality and the use of cosmetics, I try to make these missions as covert as possible. I used to sneak into my sister Andrea's room and use her makeup to cover blemishes, until she caught me one day and bought me my own stuff. I felt the need to hide my habit from the rest of my family, furtively stowing the makeup in my sock drawer, underneath my stack of *Playboy*s (sorry, Mom).

High school came and went, but the occasional blemish still cropped up. Usually they landed right between my eyes like a *bindi*. One was so bad, I contemplated telling people I'd converted to Hinduism, until a friend of mine reminded me that traditionally only women wear the *bindis*. But I eventually handled that whitehead the way my brother, Mike, taught me to handle all my zits. Wait until it ripens and then pop away. The further you can get the sucker to shoot, the better. He was always bragging about "hitting the mirror," a feat that I only accomplished once.

After popping, you dried out the area as much as possible with a product called Sea Breeze. I would douse cotton ball after cotton ball with that stuff, trying to drain all the grease off my face. The other solution was to use the zit creams. I remember the distinct tang of Oxy, which I used to cover my face with right before hopping into bed, though I always felt that the concealer was the best weapon against zits. That little bottle my sister bought me lasted a number of years, but when it ran out, I had to go to the drugstore to buy my own bottle. Walking down the cosmetics aisle was agonizing. I was so nervous; it was as if I was purchasing a grab bag full of condoms, tampons, enemas, and adult diapers. I ended up using the pharmacist's checkout line so I wouldn't have to face the looks from normal cashiers.

In college I was even more secretive about my "concealer habit." I remember dabbing away in the darkness of my fraternity's communal bathroom, quivering at the thought I'd be caught. Somehow, I never was. Now that I'm married, I've been able to drop my guard about using makeup to cover zits, which somehow I still get from time to time. I have unfettered access to Anna's makeup kit. If we run out, I can ask her to pick up some more at the store. She seems at ease with the whole idea of me poaching a little foundation in order to save face, but there's one zit tactic she can't seem to accept. She caught me leaning in close to the mirror getting ready for some major pimple propulsion and screamed, "Wait! Don't pop it or it will get so much worse. Just leave it alone!"

I'd always popped—how could I possibly stop now? Then it occurred to me that her beauty products took up a good 95 percent of the shelf space in the bathroom, and she had flawless skin herself. Maybe—just maybe—she knew what she was talking about.

To pop or not to pop? That was the question. For the answer, I called Brian Boye, the fashion and grooming director at *Men's Health* magazine. Boye confirmed that "every dermatologist I've ever talked to says *do not* pop the zit." As with most things, Anna was right, but where's the fun in that? Not popping a zit is like not picking a scab, or not scratching a bug bite. It may worsen the problem to pop it, but there's instant gratification there for the taking, especially when pus is involved. Except the stuff oozing out of a popped zit isn't pus at all. It's called sebum, which Boye describes as a "waxy substance that gets caught in the pores of your face."

Boye said he's not trying to be a party pooper in advising not to pop, but the skin on your face is one of the most sensitive areas on your whole body. Any popping will result in extreme redness and blotchiness. Furthermore, the redness won't be confined to the deflated skin around the zit, but will involve the whole surrounding area that was squeezed, pinched, and pummeled to get that pimple to fire off. Pinching to get the pop may actually enlarge the area of redness on your face, making it more noticeable.

If you must release the sebum, Boye suggested using a sterile pin to employ the "pierce and drain" technique. Should you ignore this information and pop anyway, I suggest looking for a zit that's not in the immediate line of sight. A zit underneath the hairline or covered by facial hair is a safer bet than something right between the eyes or planted squarely in the center of your chin.

Instead of popping those zits, go on the offensive with overnight zit creams. Boye confirmed these really do work, as long as they contain three main ingredients: benzoyl peroxide, salicylic acid, and sulfur. Benzoyl peroxide kills the bacteria living in that little dot on your face, but Boye pointed out that salicylic acid is the crucial ingredient that actually unclogs your pores. Lastly, products containing sulfur will help decrease the inflammation around the zit. Interestingly, Sea Breeze may be detrimental since it kills off a lot of healthy skin cells while it's killing off bacteria. If you have major acne problems, see a dermatologist, who can prescribe more powerful treatments.

Most adults have the fortune to be past their acne problems, since our body's sebum production spikes during puberty, but you might get an errant crater or two well past your teens. Since the Oxy or Clearasil in your closet may have expired back when you were studying for your SATs, Boye has heard of another effective treatment that's bound to be in your medicine cabinet: toothpaste. While I'm sure Colgate doesn't contain sulfur or benzoyl peroxide, Boye said it will effectively dry out a zit after about a half hour. Just don't leave it on overnight. Toothpaste as zit cream? Who would have guessed? Next thing you know, people will suggest using meat tenderizer for bee stings. Oh wait, that's true, too.

Snoring: What Would Rob Do?

I used to pride myself on being the only one in my family who didn't snore. While some people are lulled to sleep by crickets, I fell asleep to an atonal Sachs family symphony. Each night, our house shook with snoring, grunting, and phlegmy exhortations. They all had their own special snores. My mother and brother were both a little nasal, my father was more of a deep snorer, and my sister, well, she was all over the place. I thought I had cheated nature, but when I was ten I had my pal Vincent for a sleepover. His bloodshot eyes the next morning were all I needed to realize that I too had been born a snorer!

After this discovery, I became terribly self-conscious. At sleepovers I'd make sure I was the last to nod off. I bought those Breathe Right nasal strips, hoping they would help, but inevitably they would fall off in the middle of the night and the buzz saw would start back up again. When I went to college, I petitioned successfully for a single room, fearing that a roommate would do terrible things to me in retaliation for my nocturnal noise. When camping, I always brought my own tent and slept a good ten feet away from everyone else.

My nasal problems finally caught up with me in Europe, of all places. I'd finished studying abroad for a semester in London (more about that in chapter 5) and joined a friend for a European extravaganza. With Eurail passes in hand, we crisscrossed the continent exploring Copenhagen, Rome, Barcelona, and other cities. One night we found ourselves on a train traveling through Germany on our way to Zurich. Our budget traveling meant sharing a sleeper car with five other passengers. The sleeper was a technological marvel for its ability to squeeze six single beds into one cabin, although it was lacking in terms of personal space. On each side of the cabin were three rows of beds: a top, a middle, and a bottom bunk. That night I found myself being the schnitzel in an oversized Bavarian sandwich.

As night fell, I grew more and more anxious about my potential for snoring. With no nasal strips to aid me, I resorted to sleeping on my side. I did my best to build a berm using the pillows, sheets, and blankets, but there wasn't much room to work with. I got on my side and let the train rock me to sleep. In the morning, I woke up rested and happy, but my bedding berm was nowhere to be found. I had destroyed it in the middle of the night. I don't speak German, but as it turns out, the facial expression for "you must die" cuts across all cultures. We were off the train by the next stop.

To find out what I could have done better that fateful night, I called up a snoring expert, Dr. Murray Grossan. Dr. Grossan is a board-certified otolaryngologist and the author of the book *The Sinus Cure*. Snoring, he explained, is most often caused by a "fatty uvula" hanging off the soft palate. I had no idea what that meant, but being told that I potentially had a "fatty uvula" only made me feel even more self-conscious about my condition. Dr. Grossan explained that the uvula is floppy tissue inside your mouth that normally serves to help articulate the sound of your voice. When it gets enlarged or supersized, it can cause you to snore. He recommends losing weight for people with oversized uvulas, though he didn't mention any uvula-specific exercise to help slim it up. He confirmed that sleeping on your side is effective as well, since it helps keep another floppy thing in your mouth from getting in the way— your tongue.

Uvulas and tongues aside, Dr. Grossan said there's a whole range of things that make people snore, including a blocked nasal passage, a deviated septum (which means that piece of cartilage that separates your nostrils is out of alignment), or the very shape of your jaw. Perhaps the saddest cause of snoring is when the very tip of your nose flops down, causing a nasal blockage. Dr. Grossan's solution for this was to literally tape up your nose before going to sleep. Fortunately, nose tip droopiness normally happens to older people, so I've got some time before I need to keep a roll of duct tape on my nightstand.

Depending on the cause, treatment for snoring involves everything from getting fitted for a special mouth guard–like device that helps keep your jaw in place to getting a "pillar" procedure, which is surgery to stiffen up your soft palate. Often these more in-depth solutions are for sleep apnea, which is when you actually stop breathing while you sleep. Dr. Grossan said before you get any surgery done, you should be tested in a sleep lab to pinpoint the problem. He also suggests trying less invasive measures to see if there's any easier solution.

One thing Dr. Grossan is a big fan of is keeping the air moist. Leaving a pan of water on your dresser will help things out, though he doesn't like humidifiers, since they can get moldy. He has attached his own name to a product called Breathe Ease, a "nasal moisturizing and irrigation system." He doesn't, however, advocate using a spritz bottle directly on the face of a snoring person (I had to ask).

Another of Dr. Grossan's favorite techniques is to sew a tennis ball into the back of an old T-shirt to make you less likely to sleep on your back. Fortunately I won't need to resort to this, because Anna is more than happy to nudge me onto my side when I start snoring. Dr. Grossan told me I'm one of the lucky ones, since many wives wind up kicking or jabbing their hubbies. This rouses the snorer out of a deep sleep, which really isn't a healthy solution.

So if you're a snorer, the next time you board a sleeper car on a train, consider coming equipped with tape for your nose, a pan of water for the room, and a tennis ball for your T-shirt. Your fellow passengers may give you a few weird looks, but that's much better than the red-eyed stares you'd otherwise get in the morning.

Forget Someone's Name? What Would Rob Do?

Many of us have a recurring nightmare that always plays out the same way. There are the proverbial "flunking final exams" terrors, or the one where you show up to class completely naked. While I've had variations of these nightmares, there's also one where I return to school after summer break and discover that I've forgotten everyone's name.

Something like this really did happen to me once. I went from having eighty-two classmates in high school to a college with over two thousand freshmen. It was one of the toughest transitions of my life. I was used to knowing everyone and I was afraid I would never remember all these new names. Freshman year wasn't so bad because all the students had their names on their dormitory doors. The freshman facebook also helped. Unlike the Web site of the same name, my facebook was an actual printed glossy directory with a picture of each member of the freshman class. It was my freshman-year bible. The first few months, I would pore over it almost nightly, desperately trying to remember the hundreds of names that were whizzing by me on campus.

Studying the facebook only took me so far. There wasn't enough room in my head to memorize classmate names along with the names of Civil War battlefields in my History of the South class, or equations for calculating the distance between stars for my astronomy class. That facebook was also useless whenever I met upperclassmen. By the end of the first semester, I only knew the names of people in my immediate hall and those from high school who were also at college with me.

The stakes were higher when girls were involved. One time I was hitting on some girl at a party, and she caught on that

I'd forgotten who she was. "I'll leave this party with you if you could just do one thing for me . . . tell me my name." I knew the likelihood of getting it right was slim, so I guessed something like "Buffy" in the hopes that I'd get a laugh and maybe a little bit of forgiveness as well. That didn't work.

At times when I wasn't cornered with a direct question, I was often able to figure out a name using the ID method. Back in high school, my friends and I thought it would be hysterical to look like complete idiots in our school ID pictures. In my senior year picture, I'm posing with prop eyeglasses and a look on my face like I've just smelled some really bad gas. One guy in my class posed with a bowl of cereal for his portrait. The tradition carried over into college and would help me out of tons of jams. I'd start a conversation by saying, "Hey, have I ever shown you my ID picture?" Then I would whip out my mug shot and casually ask to see theirs. It was a great tool for not only figuring out someone else's name but also helping that other person to remember mine. This of course doesn't work if the person goes by his middle name or some random nickname.

The ID trick was one of the many forms of moniker espionage I engaged in. Sometimes I recruited a coconspirator. I'd go up to a friend and ask him to introduce himself to someone I wanted to talk to, and then ask that person's name. The only danger here is if your friend walks up to the both of you at the same time and forgets his line. Then you're obliged to introduce them without knowing the other person's name. That's when you have to slur an approximation of the other person's name: "This is Kazzzny," which at a loud college party could pass for Katie, Catherine, Kathy, Cagney, or . . . Kazny.

When nobody else has been around to help out, I've also tried getting someone to talk about her own name. I'd say something like, "I used to get made fun of all the time when I was little because people would call me names like 'Saxophone' or 'Sexy Sachs' or 'Rob my sacks of cats.'" (Okay, nobody ever used the last one.) After sharing my story, I'd ask if she ever got teased, hoping she will give me a funny story that I can use to remember her name. Or sometimes I'd inquire, "What did your family call you when you were little?" Hopefully, it won't be Princess.

If you're not so good at face-to-face reconnaissance, there are less invasive methods for procuring names. In college I used to peek in backpacks, binders, notebooks, or anything that might have a name written on it. Now you can use social Web sites like Facebook or MySpace to see if you can figure out who somebody is through your circle of friends. You can also befriend someone who is really good with names and have him act as your personal Rolodex. Another "more advanced" technique is to challenge a person to a rap battle. The trick is to begin your rhyme with the words, "My name is . . ." Mine goes something like this:

> My name is Rob,
> I'm on the job
> And though I eat with my hands,
> I ain't no slob.

Then tell her it's her turn and she needs to follow the same format. Sit back and wait for her to give up the goods.

These tricks don't always fly in a work setting (though it would be fun to rap battle with some of my coworkers). There are times when the easiest thing to do is to come clean about forgetting someone's name. Within the first thirty seconds of talking to someone, it's okay to say, "I'm an idiot and I've forgotten your name." If you're not feeling self-deprecating, a simple "Oh, remind me of your name again?" will do as well. Letting a conversation go longer than five minutes without saying that makes you not only an idiot but a jerk, since the person you're talking to thinks you've been duping him the whole conversation.

My career at NPR has taken me from Washington, D.C., to Los Angeles and back to D.C. I knew there would be a lot of people I'd recognize but whose names I'd forget. To get some new tricks for the workplace, I called memory expert Harry Lorayne. He holds memory seminars all the time and has a full line of memory-related products. He was at first reluctant to talk to me, since people usually pay a lot of money to get the information he gives. Fortunately, I got him to open up on my specific problem of forgetting names, and he gave me a few hints.

He said that most of the names we forget are ones we never heard in the first place. Many times when people tell us their names, we're not really paying attention. When you hear someone say his or her name, you have to flag it in your brain as a vital piece of information. Lorayne recommended repeating the name right away to try to commit it to memory.

Let's say you're meeting me. I'll say, "Hi, my name is Rob Sachs." You can first verify that you heard it being pronounced the right way. Say it back to me. "Rob Sachs, is that correct?" Second, you can make a quick association with the name, or start talking about it in the conversation. Ask if Sachs has any relation to Saks Fifth Avenue or Goldman Sachs. (There is none, by the way.) The more you talk about the name right away, the more likely you are to remember it.

Another possibility is to try to associate someone's name with one of his physical characteristics. For instance, if you meet someone named Ben Green and you notice he has green eyes, you can repeat that in your head. Ben Green with the green eyes. Ben who has eyes that are green. Ben's last name is Green. My trick for remembering a name like Mikhail Gorbachev would be to think of the red splotch on his head as being gory. "Gory splotch" sounds like "Gorbachev." This might be a stretch, but it can work. The idea is to have a visual cue that correlates to the name.

Lorayne said another great thing to do is to use the name as often as you can over the course of your conversation. Try to eliminate all pronouns and just say the person's name instead, while always being careful not to say the name too much, since that can be a little creepy. "So Rob, what do you think about the weather? How about those Phillies, Rob? Rob, what brings you here?" I've tried this out, and to my amazement, it works. People also appreciate hearing their own name, because it makes them feel you care about them, or are a thoughtful person.

Harry Lorayne is a pro at this. He can repeat the names of a whole roomful of people he's just met. He told me that if you practice a lot and work on it, over time you will get better at it. These techniques have already started to help me in the office, though I still have one more trick. If I didn't catch someone's name or have forgotten it, I now go to the new searchable online database of NPR employees that contains everyone's picture from their photo ID. It's my own little office facebook, and I've lost more than a few hours of productivity studying it.

I Clogged the Toilet and I'm at a Party! What Would Rob Do?

Continuing on the theme of being caught with your pants down, here's a scenario that any houseguest dreads more than any other: clogging up your host's toilet. In the past, I might have gone the simple yet shameful route of running away from the problem, but as I've matured into the man I am today, I've conquered my own inhibitions and now have a way of dealing with this mortifying predicament. I have a plumber friend (not named Joe) to thank for it.

The thing that's most horrifying about clogging a toilet is that it taps into one of our biggest fears, which is having someone else see our doody. While the act of defecation itself may offer a certain sense of gratification (or at the very least relief), knowing that its results are being whisked away down the pipes to some far-off place is even more satisfying. With every flush, there's a small part of me that says, "Yeah, there it goes!" While the excitement of seeing it all go down the drain has dissipated somewhat in my adult years, a part of me still wants to clap my hands (after I've washed them, of course) every time I flush. It only takes one trip to a Porta-Potty at a concert or sporting event to be reminded of how ugly things get without proper plumbing.

When you flush and the water rises up in protest, you're in trouble. In times of all-out horror like this, it helps to turn to religion: "Please, please, please, Almighty [fill in your higher power here], please don't let this bowl overflow."

Praying for a little miracle might not be a bad idea, because an overflowing toilet could really be worse than you'd think. According to Bob McHone, owner of Crown Plumbing and Heating based in Frederick, Maryland, if toilet water splashes down onto the floor, you run the risk of water damage to the floorboards. If a lot of water pours out, water tainted with fecal matter might start dripping through the ceiling. And if your hosts happen to have a ceiling fan underneath a second floor bathroom . . . you get the picture.

As with most disasters, prevention is the key to coming out unscathed. Older toilets or ones connected to older piping are more likely to clog. McHone recommended finding a toilet that's fully glazed and has a two-and-one-eighth-inch trapway and a three-inch flapper. You could ask your host about his toilet specs before you go, or you could take a tape measure into the bathroom with you, but it might be easier to just poke around the house before you have to go so you can scope out your throne room options. Here's what you're looking for: one, a bathroom that offers the most privacy; and, two, a modern toilet that looks like it will be able to withstand the impending bowel onslaught.

Once you've located your place of business, you still need to take precautions while you're doing the deed. You may be familiar with the term "courtesy flush," which is the flush-as-you-go method. While the original logic behind courtesy flushing is to mitigate odor, McHone said it also has a practical application in terms of clog prevention. Flushing midway through enables the toilet to consume your excrement in small bites rather than shoving one big load down its gullet. Just be prepared to wait between flushes for the bowl to fill back up with water. (This is when I'm sure you'll be glad you brought your copy of *What Would Rob Do?* in there with you.)

Even the best toilets get clogged, though, and it may not always be your fault. The woman who used the toilet before you could have flushed down a tampon, or someone's kid might have recently drowned his sister's Barbie doll head. You could be set up for this, but there's no time to point fingers when you have your pants around your ankles. It's time to take charge to make sure the poop water doesn't splash over the sides of the bowl.

Preventing an overflow is actually a lot easier than you might think. Bob McHone suggested that you first stop the water from rushing into the bowl. To do this you have to know a little bit about toilet mechanics. Fortunately, it's pretty simple. The bowl fills up with water until a little weighted floatie (no, not that kind of floatie) device gets to a predetermined level, which causes the water to shut off, usually when the tank is full of water. Flushing the toilet simply lifts up the flapper, allowing water to rush into the bowl from the tank. The flapper drops back down on its own when all the water has evacuated the tank. McHone said the quickest way to "undo" your flush is to push back down that flapper so that it "drops prematurely, so the water doesn't exit the tank."

Getting to the flapper may be easier said than done for two reasons. First, toilet tank covers can be really heavy, and there's not always a convenient place to put them once you take them off. Shattering a porcelain toilet cover on the bathroom floor after you've clogged the toilet takes things from bad to worse. Second, many people like to use the toilet cover as a shelf, piling on tissue boxes, candles, books, potpourri, Zen rock gardens, and all sorts of other knickknacks, making it nearly impossible to get in there in time to prevent a spillover. My recommendation is to take the lid off ahead of time if you're worried you're going to drop a clog-worthy deuce. That way, you can peacefully enjoy the experience and possibly stop the flapper without even getting up off the seat. Panic situation averted.

But wait! Pushing down the flapper is only the beginning. McHone said that now you have to reach down and shut off the water itself. Most toilets have a shutoff lever near the foot of the toilet, that lovely area with the pee stains, where little dust bunnies collect. If you're feeling squeamish about getting on your hands and knees, try thinking about your cauldron of colon chowder for motivation.

If you've gotten this far, you'll notice you still haven't fully taken care of the problem. Yes, you may have prevented an overflow, but there's still the issue of those little guys (or that one big sucker) still floating around in the bowl. You can almost hear them taunting you—"Ha, ha, ha, we're still here!" They must be flushed. This is when you reach for the plunger. A good host will have one within reach, or hiding just out of sight somewhere in the bathroom—in a closet or under the sink. Search it out. As a last resort, go out and ask your host for one. Just leave a sign on the door that says DO NOT ENTER, or CLOSED FOR RENOVATION. Remember, at all costs, don't let anyone else see your poop. It's one image that they'll never forget—ever.

Once you've secured a plunger, fill up the bowl with water. I know it sounds crazy, but the plunger needs liquid to be effective, since the plunging works not when you're pushing down, but when you're pulling up. McHone said the best technique is to slowly push in and then jerk out the plunger swiftly. If you do things right, a plunger alone will do the trick the majority of the time.

If this doesn't work, you might have to cut your losses. You could tape a note to the plunger that says, "Sorry, I tried." At least your host will know that you gave it a good fight.

Got Clutter? What Would Rob Do?

"Slobbie Robbie." Ever since I was a kid, my family has been calling me that. I never liked the nickname, but to be honest, I deserved it. On the low end of the scale, my room was a "wreck-a-roony," playfully messy. At its worst, my room was "an abomination," which meant I was in for a night of cleaning.

I didn't intentionally keep my room messy out of some act of defiance. I was the victim of nature. I was born with two personality traits that led me to be this way. One was being psychologically predisposed to not putting things back after I finished using them. My father says the medical term for this is something called "laziness." The other personality trait was that I had too big a heart, too much love inside of me, which made it hard to throw away things that had touched my life in some deep, emotional way. My mother had a hard time seeing why I felt the need to keep movie stubs, old birthday cards, shopping receipts, and menus from various restaurants piled on my desk.

I also had a habit of picking up every brochure I could find because they were free. Once I went through an almanac that contained the numbers of regional tourist offices, and I systematically called up each one to request my free visitor's brochure from every state. That was the only time I ever got a letter from the state of North Dakota. While the mail piled up, I totally lacked the organizational skills to deal with it. Compounding the problem was that the longer things stuck around, the more they grew in sentimental value. What one month was an empty bubble gum wrapper, two years later became the last memento from the huge tub of Dubble Bubble that my brother Mike got from his bar mitzvah—oh, the memories.

My first breakthrough in eliminating paper clutter came in the form of a corkboard. I realized that small items like meaningful bubble gum wrappers could be neatly pinned up at eye level and be protected from my mother's periodic clean sweeps. She would go through and painstakingly tidy up my entire room, a feat that I should have praised her for but instead complained about because my personal space had been violated. Only later did I learn that if I wanted to hide something, I had to bury it in Mike's room.

Eventually it became difficult to find any spare cork on the corkboard. Things began to pile up vertically. That's when I made breakthrough number two: scrapbooking. I know what you're thinking. Dude, did you say scrapbooking? I did, and I'm not ashamed. Now, I didn't go crazy with it and start using lacy paper or Bedazzlers or anything like that. But I found that gluing all my ticket stubs together on one page of a cheap photo album was a good way to keep track of them. The whole scrapbooking thing also helped with my pack-rat problem. Gluing things down took effort, which in effect raised the bar on what scraps I wanted to keep around. Goodbye, Montana Visitor's Guide.

Even as a bachelor, I hobbled along for years with a quasi-effective system of letting my room turn into a "pig sty" (to use Mom's vernacular) and then rushing to clean up as fast as possible whenever a lady friend was on her way over. This continued until I was living in Los Angeles, where a friend told me about a company called Garage Specialists, which is devoted to cleaning up people's messy garages. They also try to help people develop better habits so they don't find themselves back in the same old clutter situation months later. Their motto is: "The first step to inner peace is a clean garage." Garage Specialists was founded by Jonathan Marder, a guy who saw a way to turn his organizational skills into a profitable business. Turns out garage cleaning can be lucrative—a typical job can run anywhere from a few hundred bucks to thousands of dollars. I visited Marder on a job site with satirist Brian Unger for a story we were working on. When we arrived, Marder and his crew were sorting through a garage stuffed with everything from toys to yellowing magazines to old videocassettes. He told us exercise gear and old tripods are the two most common things he finds cluttering up a garage, but he's also come upon more naughty items such as sex toys and drug paraphernalia. Marder has even unearthed a woolly mammoth's tooth and a pair of shellacked bull testicles (funny, I thought those normally get bronzed).

After hanging out with Marder, I relayed to him my own struggles with the clutter demons. Like many others, Marder diagnosed me as suffering from a pack-rat mentality, which makes me hold on to every item I've ever possessed out of fear that I might one day have a need for it again. I told him about my scrapbooking system, which he thought was good, but he also warned that some "clutterers" are people who have too many systems for keeping things straight. "These are people who are in some ways overorganized . . . creating lists about the lists they need to do and need to take care of." If only I had known about that argument growing up. I would love to have seen the look on my mother's face when I told her, "The problem isn't that I'm not trying to be clean, it's that I'm trying too hard to be clean!"

Marder said I needed a support system to help me break my clutter habits. He called it finding a "clutter friend" or "clutter pal." I like to think of this person as a "clutter buddy." In my bachelor days, finding a clutter buddy might have been a difficult proposition. It's tough enough to get someone to drive you to the airport, let alone asking a guy to come over and help you clean up your place, or catalog your CD collection. This is when you need to call on the opposite sex—or in my case, remind Anna that she swore to stand by me in sickness and in health. My clutter problem is definitely a sickness. In addition, my space is now her space, ergo my clutter is now her clutter. As Marder explained, Anna's job as a "clutter buddy" is not to clean up my mess, but to help me figure out how to do it myself.

Soon after we moved in together I realized that sharing a space with a woman is not a fifty-fifty proposition in terms of how much stuff you get to keep. It's more like thirty-seventy (if you're lucky). That's not to say I don't get to keep any of my junk. I still have the plastic trophy I won for eating a one-and-a-half-pound tsunami burger from Top Dog Café in Hatteras Island, North Carolina. I also have on display some of the less-than-stellar prizes I've accumulated from state fairs (see "Winning Carnival Games" in chapter 2). Anna has also stepped up my scrapbooking game. Now my movie stubs are splayed out across the page in an artistic pattern.

Every once in a while, things still get out of control. Fortunately, Marder also shared advice for how to attack a room full of mess. He said that while sorting through your things, you want to "make aisles, not piles." Instead of throwing your belongings into a heap in the corner, find a way to organize them so that you can put things away as a group. Anna came up with the idea of using a bag designated for each room in the house. When she's cleaning up, she drops things that belong in a different room into the bag so she can bring them all back together.

Marder also suggested creating what he called a "dedicated dumping zone" (DDZ). The DDZ is a place where you can shove things guilt-free when you haven't figured out where to put them yet. Growing up, my mother gave me a DDZ called the "junk drawer." DDZs are great, except that I never made it to Marder's next step, which is to systematically weed through your DDZ and find a place to put things permanently. Even now when I go back to visit my parents, I see stuff in the old junk drawer that I should have thrown out in 1987.

Perhaps the most valuable tip Marder gave me was to learn how to have an objective voice. In other words, take time to detach yourself from objects. To do so, you'll really need to lean on your clutter buddy. Marder urges clutter buddies to evaluate the other person's items and make the tough decisions *for* them. While that may sound brutal, Anna and I have found a way to make it work for us. We allow each other to have veto power so the other doesn't throw out an item that we feel particularly strongly about. (Somehow I forgot to invoke this with my poor old lava lamp. I really miss that thing.)

Anna has even made this weeding-out process into a game. Once or twice a year, we have a big "in-house" fashion show where we model our whole wardrobe for each other. The other person then gets to decide if clothes stay or go. It's a great way to take the sentimentality out of keeping clothes. With Anna's help, I finally evicted all of the hand-me-down Polo knit shirts from the '90s that my brother gave me, and for the first time I finally saw the bottom of my dresser drawer. It also felt nice giving those shirts a better home at Goodwill.

Cohabitation hasn't cured me of all my clutter problems. I still leave clothes on the floor and let papers pile up from time to time, but I have gotten better. I think Anna and I have a shared desire not to gross each other out by being too sloppy. I've learned that the more times I toss my boxers in the laundry hamper, the less chance I'll have of seeing a sports bra lying around.

With a new baby, it's hard to stay on top of all the cleaning all the time, so Anna and I have employed one last important cleaning lesson from Jonathan Marder and the Garage Specialists: we pay someone to do it for us. Twice a month a housekeeper comes to clean and organize. We still do a ton of housework ourselves, but we both appreciate not having to scrub the toilet and shower. There's nothing I enjoy more these days than coming home to see all my stuff neat and tidy, especially if it's on a day when my parents are visiting.

Protecting Your Voice: What Would Rob Do?

I used to think that losing your voice was the coolest thing you could do. What other way could you show that you'd really partied hard or had the most awesome time at a concert besides sounding raspy the next day? It was a hoarse badge of courage, and the ramifications for impaired vocal cords were minimal. At worst, I would have to stop singing Foreigner songs full blast in the shower for a couple of days.

Even joining NPR didn't curtail my propensity to scream in manic joy while watching bands like the Red Hot Chili Peppers or Rage Against the Machine. Anti-authoritarian lyrics aren't meant to be whispered, and I actually liked the age-bump I got with a little extra scratch in my voice. Unlike my former colleague Bob Edwards, whose Marlboro Red Kentucky basso profundo makes you kowtow to his authority, my barely post-pubescent shrill—while endearing to my wife—sometimes leaves telemarketers asking to speak to my father when I answer the phone. That said, if a whiny Ira Glass can be a public radio star, can't that guy who sounds too young to be on the air find a home too?

Now that I'm a little older, I realize it's not wise to damage your voice when you've chosen a career in radio. Some of my colleagues at NPR are very careful with their vocal cords, even sipping warm water or whispering when they're not on the air. To get the best advice on protecting your voice, I figured

I should ask someone who's paid to shout at the top of her lungs—a professional opera singer named Jennifer Wilson.

First, Wilson dispelled the myth that the tea-with-lemon thing is helpful. Caffeine dries out your vocal cords, so she makes a point of staying away from coffee or other drinks with caffeine. While caffeine is out for her, supplements are not. Wilson takes 200 to 400 milligrams of coenzyme Q_{10} per day, which she said helps boost her immunity.

Second, Wilson uses a humidifier wherever she can, because a moist environment equals happy vocal cords. When traveling out West, she uses something called a swamp cooler, and if she can't find one, Wilson spends a few minutes standing over steaming manhole covers (okay, I made that up, but I think it could be effective in a pinch). And if you'll allow me another aside, my father recommends steam baths for clearing out your lungs, which he also likes to tout as the perfect spot to exfoliate your feet. In any case, Wilson recommends breathing in humid air wherever you can find it.

Third, Wilson avoids speaking as much as she can. "Many actors don't speak any word that they're not being paid for," she said, "and for singers, it's sort of the same thing because our voice is our livelihood." She avoids loud bars and restaurants, excuses herself from concerts or sporting events where she might have to shout, and even polices her personal relationships by refusing to be lured into potential arguments. On the whole, she becomes much more acquiescent. "A wardrobe lady used to say that she loved working with opera singers because they never yell at you," Wilson said.

Since operas are so expensive to produce, if Wilson were to lose her voice, the show would have to go on, even if they were without understudies. Wilson told me this famous story (famous in the opera world, that is) of how during one performance of

La Bohème, the actor who played Marcello had to sing both his role and the part of another actor who had lost his voice, even though they had some scenes together. How did he do it? The mute actor would mime out his part while the actor playing Marcello would sing the words from behind a book or another prop.

It's good to know I'll never have to put my voice through that kind of workout, except when I need to perform both parts of the duet of "(I've Had) the Time of My Life" alone in the shower.

Getting Fit and Losing Weight: What Would Rob Do?

Before I start talking about losing weight, let's be clear: I'm not a big guy. At first glance, most people would consider me in shape. Yet take a second look at my belly, and you may just notice a hint of pudge; nothing crazy, but definitely there's some gelatinous-like movement going on with my gut. It started with what's called "sympathy weight"—when a guy gains weight during his wife's pregnancy. Perhaps I overindulged when I joined Anna in her root-beer-float cravings. But even after our daughter was born, I realized that while I'm not gaining more weight, I'm not really losing much either.

My experience jibes with a study done in 2004 by researchers at Duke University, which shows that men on average have a 4 percent increase in obesity risk after each child (there's a 7 percent increase for women). While it makes me feel somewhat better knowing that I'm not alone, it doesn't change the fact that when I look at my wardrobe I see a couple of things that don't fit anymore.

The Duke study cites decrease in activity as well as less time to prepare healthy meals as the main causes of this after-child weight gain. While I think Anna and I are doing a good job of eating healthy, we've both decreased the amount of exercise we get these days. When I was in my midtwenties and single, and I had a job that allowed me to train in the mornings before work, I used to run a lot. In fact, when a friend asked me to join him in signing up for a marathon, I didn't think twice. These days my life looks much different. My workday begins when it's still dark out, and when I get home it's time to play with my daughter. Workout time never got factored into this new lifestyle.

Slowly becoming a slouch is no fun, but what makes it harder is that I'm related to a fitness fanatic. My brother, Mike, works out five times a week and religiously monitors his diet down to the last morsel he puts in his mouth. Ironically, he never cooks for himself (unless you call blending a protein shake cooking), but he knows a lot about maintaining a healthy lifestyle. He's one of those guys who can make their pecs move up and down, and he's more than happy to show you this trick. My pecs are nicely hidden by an abundance of chest hair, so that would never work for me anyway.

Getting back to my gut . . . When I asked Mike for his advice on getting in shape, he said all I needed to know was one name: Mark Rippetoe. Mike said that Rippetoe changed his whole philosophy of fitness, and that there is a whole movement growing behind him.

I called up Rippetoe at his gym, Crossfit Wichita, in Wichita Falls, Texas. He has over twenty-five years of experience coaching elite athletes in strength and fitness training and is the author of *Starting Strength: Basic Barbell Training*, a book Mike tells me completely shifted his perspective on weight training. It didn't take long for me to understand why Mike liked Rippetoe so much. The man gets to the point when it comes to what he thinks works and doesn't work with exercise. For instance, when I asked him about the effectiveness of aerobic workouts (treadmills, elliptical machines) for losing weight, he said, "If that actually worked, then everybody in the gym that's on that equipment would not be fat."

Rippetoe said that "muscle burns fat for fuel, and if you ultimately want to affect the amount of body fat you've got, you have to affect your muscle mass, and the only way to affect your muscle mass is by doing exercise that challenges the ability of that muscle mass to produce force, and that is resistance training." This means pumping iron. Ugh.

I've only lifted weights consistently once in my life, and that's because it was a requirement for my high school gym class. With that in mind, I asked Rippetoe if there was another way to get a good workout, perhaps with a rowing machine? I figured Rippetoe would advocate these devices, since it was a rowing machine that once inflicted upon me the most pain I've ever felt in a gym. Rippetoe conceded that rowing machines are the exception to his rule about aerobic equipment, but unfortunately most gyms don't have them.

If rowing was somewhat effective, perhaps a few outdoor sports could also get me out of the weight room. I told Rippetoe how a few months of really intense basketball playing had once given me stronger muscles and better endurance. He wasn't impressed. He said I felt stronger because I started from a place of being unfit, and that eventually I would plateau. Rippetoe told me that if I wanted to see my strength and fitness grow, I needed to be on a resistance-training program.

Rippetoe said you don't need to bother with fancy gym equipment. "You can do every exercise that you'll ever need to do for the rest of your life with a barbell and a set of plates, a power rack, and a flat bench," he said, and he recommended the squat as the single best exercise for your exercise routine. "Learning how to squat will make more difference in your appearance over a shorter period of time than any single thing you can do. You have to learn how to squat correctly, correctly being below parallel." When squatting, make sure you get help from someone you trust (who may or may not be the gym's personal trainer—Rippetoe is leery of them too).

Mike is a big squatter. I know this because he's often made me accompany him to the gym to watch him perform them. After watching a couple of reps, I figured out why people ask, "How much can you bench?" rather than "How much can you squat?" People look good while benching. Even if they're grunting, they still look cool. The look on the face of a squatter seems to be one of extreme anguish and severe constipation.

I think I'd prefer to save face by watching my diet a little more closely and buying a rowing machine. I'll leave the squatting to Mike. Sorry, big brother, you'll have to grunt alone. But if it's any consolation, you'll always have bigger muscles than I do.

Passing Gas: What Would Rob Do?

If there's one issue that stands out as the quintessential *What Would Rob Do?* indignity, it's flatulence: passing gas, farting, beefing, or "letting a fluffy." It's something that happens to everyone (and to some of us, it happens more often than we'd like to admit). On average, people trouser bark fourteen times a day, according to the National Institute of Diabetes and

Digestive and Kidney Diseases. (Sounds like a fun place to work, right?) That "comes out" to somewhere between one and three pints of gas daily (gross, isn't it?). For those with irritable bowel syndrome (IBS), it can get a lot worse. IBS sufferers can pass gas hundreds of times a day, virtually all day long. It can be very uncomfortable and unpleasant for them, not to mention hard to hide.

For most of us, passing gas is something we do on the sly. It's amazing more people don't get caught in the act. If everyone farts fourteen times a day, and you work in an office with, say, twenty other people, you've got literally hundreds of fluffies people are trying to snuff out during business hours.

Most adults will do anything to conceal their toots. For kids, it's the complete opposite. When I was in summer camp, we'd slurp down beans to make ourselves fart all night in the bunks. I remember being frustrated if I couldn't join in the nightly bout of chemical warfare. As I got older and my stink bombs elicited more displeasure than amusement from those around me, I started to find more discreet ways to deal with my gas. I used techniques such as the Duck and Cover, the Clench and Wince, and the somewhat shameful Release and Blame. I was good at keeping my gas to myself, with one glaring exception. I was on a coed camping trip the summer before tenth grade, and one night around the campfire, I somehow managed to coax not one but two little hotties into sitting on my lap. I still didn't possess my driver's license, but with one girl on each knee I might as well have been the owner of a Camaro decked out with a golden wingspan. It was awesome . . . until the weight of their bodies sank into my thighs. My quads were under pressure and my butt muscles were feeling some serious strain as well. Little did I know that I was just a hair trigger away from firing off a stink bomb. Someone made a stupid comment about me being a pimp daddy, and I laughed the tiniest of guffaws. That was all it took.

Zzzzwwwip! It wasn't the loudest fart I've ever emitted, but judging by the way both those girls sprang off me, it may as well have been an air horn. The whole group was staring at me. Someone shouted, "Rob farted!" The guys all snickered while the girls looked mortified, as if they couldn't believe how gross I was. I retreated back to my tent and didn't emerge until morning. Needless to say, I was unsuccessful with the females for the rest of the trip, but oddly enough, the incident earned me some cred with the guys.

As a mature adult, I can say it's much harder to parlay flatulence into respect from your peers. I've been working on techniques to keep my gas on lockdown while in public; and after researching what causes flatulence, I'm watching my diet more closely. You probably remember that rhyme, "Beans, beans, the magical fruit, the more you eat, the more you toot." Beans pack a large amount of a complex sugar known as raffinose. Because human stomachs don't contain the necessary enzymes to break down raffinose, it shoots straight to your small intestine, where bacteria turn it into fart fuel, a nasty brew of gas-causing fermented carbohydrates.

In general, if you want to minimize your flatulence, stay away from foods like broccoli, cabbage, and high-fiber substances such as bran. Beware of tooty fruits like pears, prunes, and peaches. If you develop lactose intolerance, dairy foods such as ice cream, milk shakes, cheese, and sour cream can be devastating (though products like Lactaid may help). I used to think drinking soy milk was a good alternative to regular milk, but soy can also cause gas. Watch out for soda and beer, as the air bubbles in them that sometimes make you belch can also find their way out the rear exit. While we're talking about air, a lot of gas is simply the result of swallowing too much air while you're eating. Mundane activities like chewing gum, sipping through a straw, or sharing a hookah at the Middle Eastern café can lead to an unpleasant outcome.

Some foods actually help eliminate flatulence. Papaya is known as nature's gas stopper. That's good news if you live in Jamaica or Hawaii, but those of us who don't live in a tropical locale aren't always able to get papaya into our diet. Your drugstore's a lot closer than an island getaway, and it's where you can find options like Gas-X, which uses a chemical called simethicone. This is an antifoaming agent that makes the gas bubbles bigger in your body so you can pass them more easily by consolidating all your smaller farts into one big fart bomb. Yuck.

As an alternative to drugs, I came across the GasBGon flatulence filter. Company cofounder Sharron Huza explained to me the fundamentals of using this not-so-complex system. It's a seat cushion that you can toot on and its filter absorbs the odor, though GasBGon doesn't completely stifle the noise factor. Another thing to remember is to get out of the whole "lifting up" habit. Huza said proper technique is to "plant feet, remove plastic, place your tush on the opposite side of the zipper, sit and rip." GasBGon also makes underwear, "odor control nether garments," that run sixty-five dollars a pair. That might be a small price to pay if it saves you from stinking up your two o'clock meeting with Wendy in accounting.

Prevention and concealment are one thing, but sooner or later the odds are that you're going to get caught tooting. Realize it's perfectly acceptable to excuse yourself after you pass gas, just as you would after burping. Many of you probably have been aware of this for quite some time, but it took a while for me to get that memo. It's even possible to fart and then reprimand *someone else* for being immature. Throw in a very curt "excuse me" after you rip one, then use your eyes to dare the other person to snicker. You may have beefed out a burrito's worth of gas, but if they laugh, they're the ones being uncouth. Ha!

Combing the Coif: What Would Rob Do?

Although I find myself to be more adventurous than the average guy, I've had a conservative run of hair styles through the years. One reason being, my mother would never let me do anything crazy like get a "rattail" or shave my name into my head. But the bigger reason is that I have a "Jewfro." Not a full-blown Eugene Levy perm-type thing, but my hair has a density that gives it an uncanny poofiness. It doesn't grow long, it grows big, rising farther and farther from my skull in a tangle of curls. My first lesson in taming the Jewfro came at sleepaway camp when I was nine. A hairstylist showed up one day, giving out free haircuts. I was so excited that I sprinted across three baseball fields to be first. I knew exactly what I was going to do! *Predator*, starring Arnold Schwarzenegger with sharp, spiky hair, was *the* movie then, and I decided I wanted a spiky hairdo too.

The stylist, who had to go through about two hundred rambunctious boys, worked quickly using an electric razor. In a matter of minutes, my hair was defying gravity. What I later realized was that she had used a considerable amount of product that afternoon. When I woke up the next day, my spikes were gone, but I liked how the short length tamed the beast that lived on my scalp. "Bring on the buzz" became my new haircut motto, and I would ask for a "number four," the number setting on the electric razor (five being the longest, one being a

buzz cut). The perfect length was "short but combable," which
got me all the way through to college until I made one unfortunate mistake. I chose the wrong barber.

It was at that time that I discovered the amazing experience
of a straight-blade sideburn shave. Watching a barber sharpen
his blade on a leather strop was the second coolest thing to
observe in these joints (the first being the *Playboys* in the waiting
area). Thinking only old-school barbershops had those magical
straight blades, I went out of my way to get my haircuts in these
kinds of establishments, which, as it turns out, have their fair
share of senile barbers.

One time the guy cutting my hair had spectacles that were
thicker than bulletproof glass. I asked for my usual style: setting number four on the top. He used the number four setting
on the top but went to the number two setting on the sides,
giving me an uneven look that was prevalent among skat-
ers back then. Now, I don't mind the sides and back being
shorter than the top, but I prefer a graduated flow from short
to shorter on the noggin. When I asked him to "even things
out" he whipped out the electric razor again, and moments
later I looked like an enlisted soldier. When my parents came
for a visit, my mother saluted me.

I went off electric shears after that and became a scissors-
only man, then slid into being a "Why cut my hair at all?" guy.
When I moved to Los Angeles I decided to completely free the
'fro and my hair grew . . . and grew . . . and grew. I rediscovered
curls I hadn't had since I was three years old. I felt my personality emerging from the top of my head. It was all so exciting,
so California.

Having long hair meant it needed a lot of upkeep. Taming
it became a daily battle. I scoured the pharmacy aisles for hair
gel, styling cream, hair paste, anything that could mat down my

mop, and then I dared it to pop up on me. It was a good look when it worked, but somehow that rat's nest always seemed brash enough to defy whatever product I used. Did other guys go through the same agony? Wasn't there an easier way? As it happened, a work assignment would land me in the salon chair of a hair guru, Dean Banowetz. Banowetz, the self-described "Hollywood Hair Guy," works on *American Idol* and is the man behind Ryan Seacrest's coif. He was the perfect subject for one of Brian Unger's "Unger Reports," so one afternoon Brian decided to put my curls into Banowetz's hands.

First, Banowetz took out a straightening iron, which sizzled every time it touched my follicles. In about a half hour, my curls were near comatose and rigor mortis had set in. For the first time in my life, my hair was completely straight. It felt like I was wearing a wig made of my own hair. We took before and after pictures. People said I looked mean with straight hair. I thought I kind of looked like Axl Rose (pre-braids, of course).

Banowetz didn't just give me a new look, he also gave me some great advice. For starters, never pick a random barber or stylist off the street. "To go into somewhere cold turkey, that could be disastrous," he said. He suggested looking at hair-styles on other people, and when you see one you like, ask that person who cuts their hair. Stopping random strangers to inquire about their salon choices may be awkward, though, so start with your coworkers.

Banowetz is also a fan of adding color. Caramel highlights, he told me, would go a long way toward sprucing up my look. I had one experience with highlights, which involved dumping Kool-Aid in my hair one summer, but I wasn't game on revis-iting that look. Banowetz also suggested trying out different styling products as the best way to experiment on your hair. He said the rule of thumb is, the thicker the hair, the thicker the gel or paste or pomade you'll need. As for the straightening iron, I actually enjoyed trying out something different for a short time, since the Axl Rose look only lasted a day. The next shower I took reanimated my curls.

Ultimately, whether it's by accident, by experimentation, or in the name of journalism, changing your hairdo once in a while is usually a good thing. If you wind up hating your new look, just remind yourself that you're not limited to a single style. I do my hair in a variety of styles now, and even my mother has come around toward accepting, even liking, my many different looks—well, the ones I allow her to see, at least.

5.

Slipups in the Spotlight

Most of us don't have a deep-seated need to be validated by the opinions of strangers. Unfortunately, I'm not like most people. No matter what public situation I'm in, I feel it's my duty to provide a good show, and I always aim to please. I'm a natural ham. Growing up, I owned the stage during the brief intermission between the main course and dessert of our family dinners. I did everything from impressions to miming to mimicking a fisherman being overwhelmed by a big catch. (Why? I have no idea.) Outside the home, I performed in summer camp plays and high school talent shows. The fact that I lacked any real astonishing talents didn't faze me in the least.

As a young NPR employee, I was tasked with doing the grunt work of booking guests, editing audio, and finding tape for others who were on air. So when an opportunity came to appear on NPR's big morning news broadcast *Morning Edition*, I seized it. One night while I was working late, a story came in from South America. It was a serious news report about a town that had been devastated by a natural disaster. Most of the sound bites collected for the story were from local farmers speaking Spanish. Since radio doesn't have the benefit of subtitles, the network gets around the language barrier by playing a few seconds of the quote in Spanish, then lowering the volume and running it underneath an English translation. The piece needed a young male English speaker to be the translation voice. I was around, so they picked me. The script was two sentences long, but I took six takes to get through it. I wanted to get the inflection just right. I tried to sound sad and really distraught, and threw in a hint of an accent to lend a little more "authenticity."

Lying in bed when the piece aired the next morning, I smiled from ear to ear as I heard my first on-air lines on national radio. I was still beaming when I arrived in the office later that day. My boss, the senior producer of the show, wasn't as enthused. Translated audio is to be simply recited, not acted out, I learned. Apparently, some of our Spanish-speaking listeners did not appreciate my performance. From that day forward, *Morning Edition* adopted a new official policy for translations known as the ABR rule, or "Anybody But Rob."

I've been on the air many times as a reporter since my days at *Morning Edition*, but I think I still have that acting bug buried in me. Living in D.C. offers ample opportunity to get involved in community theater or find a role in a local production, but before I tried out for anything, I'd need to get some advice from a real thespian. For this, I called up two-time Tony Award nominee Tom Wopat—you may know him better as Luke Duke from the 1980s TV series *The Dukes of Hazzard*. These days his Broadway career has taken center stage, but to me he'll always be "just a good ol' boy."

Sometimes just encountering someone famous makes you feel like you're in the spotlight. This is what happened to me one time when I was in the Reno airport and Erik Estrada, aka Officer Frank Poncherello of the beloved 1970s and early 1980s police drama *CHiPs* walked by. Do I go crazy and gush about my *CHiPs*-themed sixth birthday party, or do I play it cool and give him some space? When a celebrity is in your midst, you may only have a split second to engage or ignore, and it's a choice you may have to live with forever (unless, of course, you do a podcast on not losing an opportunity to talk to a celebrity—then you can book an interview with him). This is exactly what I did with "Ponch," and I'll tell you what he told me I should have done.

Of course, the spotlight shines brightly on singers as well. Increasingly bars and pubs have become performance venues since karaoke invaded America's shores. It fulfills all those type-A personalities who find no greater pleasure than in singing Alicia Keys off-key to a room full of strangers. While these yahoos may not be melodious, they can sure be fun to laugh at—that is, until your buddy slips your name onto the sign-up sheet and peer pressure forces your tone-deaf butt up on stage. I talked to a "KJ," or "karaoke jockey," at one of L.A.'s most popular sing-along clubs to figure out which songs are the best bets to save you from complete humiliation.

Perhaps the most difficult performance to give is the wedding speech, a time-honored tradition. If you don't have a lot of public speaking experience, giving a wedding speech can be terrifying. Upping the degree of difficulty is the fact that these speeches need to be simultaneously gracious, funny, witty, and concise. It's a tall order, so I called stand-up comics Randy and Jason Sklar, two guys who know all about timing out one-liners, for some survival strategies.

And what could be more unnerving than performing a wedding toast? Your high school reunion. Screw things up here, and you'll have to wait another ten years for a chance at redemption. I talked to a reunion expert who helped me figure out how to prepare for that big night.

This chapter also examines two micro "onstage" moments. The first is when you leave voicemail messages. Being able to express yourself in a succinct and cogent way is a real skill that's harder to master than you might think. I talked to the king of voicemail messages, NPR's Carl Kasell. The other instance is when you're communicating online. When you're out in cyberspace, you have the ability to embarrass yourself to all your known acquaintances with just a click of the mouse. I talked to an expert gadget blogger on how to negotiate your online identity.

Lastly, I take a look at the spotlight that shines on you whenever you travel abroad and become an ambassador for all Americans. I don't recall much from the courses that I studied when I spent a semester abroad, but what not to do when you're an American in London is firmly ingrained in my head.

Performing Onstage? What Would Rob Do?

It's fair to say that my time as a child actor was extremely limited. My first role was as King Ahasuerus in *A Purim Story* put on by my nursery school class at Beth Sholom. Then came the role of Simeon in *Joseph and the Amazing Technicolor Dreamcoat* at Mah-Kee-Nac, an all-boys' sleepaway camp. The next summer I played an Oompa-Loompa in the camp's production of *Willy Wonka Jr.*, a role that required painting my face orange and dressing up in green tights. By the way, if you're already being teased by the other guys in your bunk (they were all from Long Island and I was from Philly), dressing up as an Oompa-Loompa really doesn't help. I left camp that year with a bruised ego and a disdain for theater. After that summer, my acting career went on a ten-year hiatus.

I eventually returned to the stage my sophomore year in high school. The play that spring was Shakespeare's *Julius Caesar*. I signed up, read a few lines in audition, and landed the coveted role of Soldier Number II. Then I looked further down the casting sheet and saw that my name was also next to the role of Pindarus! (Did I mention I went to a small high school?) For those who may not be familiar with this absolutely pivotal character, Pindarus is Cassius's servant who gives him bad information about Mark Antony's troops. Cassius in turn believes he's doomed, so he asks Pindarus to help him commit suicide. It all goes down in one scene (Act Five, Scene Three) which took me about a month to memorize.

I think this is a good time to mention that other members of the cast thought it more "authentic" to do Shakespeare in a British accent. I followed along using the only British accent I could do—my Cockney one, of course. Below are Pindarus's lines as written by Mr. Shakespeare:

> Fly further off, my lord, fly further off;
> Mark Antony is in your tents, my lord.
> Fly, therefore, noble Cassius, fly far off.

And here are the lines as uttered by Mr. Sachs:

> Floy footh-uh oof, me lawd, floy footh-uh oof;
> Mahk Ahn-tuh-nee is in yer tints, me lawd.
> Floy, deer-ful, nibble Cah-see-us, floy foh oof.

I don't know why no one bothered to correct me, but I knew something was wrong when people in the audience were still snickering after Cassius committed suicide. To this day, that scene has been canonized by my family as one of my top ten most mockable moments.

Let's not forget my role as Soldier II. I had no idea which side I was on. Any time soldiers were needed on stage, I would appear. This completely perplexed my parents, as in one scene I was fleeing Mark Antony's troops, and in the next I was part of his forces. It made for an unintentional subplot. Had I defected? Was I a spy? Was I really my own evil twin brother? I left that for the audience to decide. At least that role didn't require me to say any lines.

If I ever reappear on stage, I know I'll need help. I consulted my five-year-old self and went to the best actor I could think of: Tom Wopat, or Luke Duke from *The Dukes of Hazzard*. I was infatuated with that show. It had everything a boy could want: a fast car, two cool guys in lead roles, and a sweet paternal figure, old Uncle Jesse. (I didn't appreciate Daisy Duke until I got older.) The Dukes were a big part of the Friday night ritual for my brother, my sister, and me. We'd light Shabbat candles, eat roast chicken and noodle kugel with our cousins, then run out to the den to watch Luke and his cousin Bo get the best of Boss Hogg and Roscoe P. Coltrane. When that red Warner Brothers logo came on at the end of the show's credits, it was time to go to bed. I was so obsessed with this show that I even asked to have a *Dukes*-themed birthday party, which included, yes, *Dukes of Hazzard* party hats.

These days Wopat has refocused on his theater career, where he's had success in a number of Broadway productions. When I caught up with him, he was rehearsing his part as Tom Hurley in *A Catered Affair*, a role that garnered him his second Tony nomination. I asked Wopat what advice he'd give a novice thespian to avoid stinking on stage. He sees acting as a team sport, and good actors will help out those in need. "The main thing is to not abandon [each other]," he told me. A good actor won't feed you your lines but assists a struggling thespian by keeping things moving to help you get back on track.

Wopat says that the more you immerse yourself in the character, the more you can focus your attention on the stage and not on the audience. One of his most difficult theater experiences occurred when he was in a cabaret and had to play himself. With no character to hide behind, he felt a lot more pressure and personal scrutiny coming from the crowd. Immersing yourself in a character with an accent or a costume is a way to clear your head, because the audience is judging the character, not you. Maybe that horrible Cockney accent I used in *Julius Caesar* wasn't such a bad thing to do after all? No, wait . . . it was bad.

When it comes to knowing your lines, something Wopat stresses, you can do yourself a big favor by knowing your role and the context of what you are supposed to be doing. This way, if you get in trouble, you can ad-lib in a way that sounds authentic to your character. Thinking back to my difficulties with my role as Soldier II, I can now see that not knowing the context tripped me up. More than that, I had no idea what Pindarus's speech meant. I remember spending weeks trying to learn the awkward phrasing of lines like, "So I am free yet would not so have been." I still have no clue what that means. But even if I did comprehend what I was saying, ad-libbing Shakespeare was out of the question. I mean, I couldn't just say, "Fly further off my lord, get on out of here." But Wopat warns that even if you're not reading text written by the world's greatest playwright, you want to be careful with ad-libbing too much. He advises "not to use [it] as a crutch" and to stay away from being "too self-indulgent" on-stage. Trying to make up your own zingers for the audience may win you a few laughs but will get you a lot of grief from the other actors, not to mention the playwright.

Wopat's last piece of advice is one I'd never considered. He says it's important for actors to stay fit and healthy because act-ing is physically demanding. Wopat likes to hit the gym four or five times a week so he can stay agile and fresh. Acting is about breaking a leg, not pulling a hammy. I appreciated Wopat's time and advice, though I'm kicking myself for chickening out and not asking about how he mastered getting into a car by sliding in through the window (it's a Bo and Luke thing).

As far as my future career on stage is concerned, perhaps I'll find a compelling role in a community theater production or a fun part in a parent-night skit when my daughter is in preschool. I think I'd like to try out for a musical too, since memorizing songs seems a lot easier than trying to remember whole monologues. How about a musical based on *The Dukes of Hazzard*? Now *that* would be something worth coming out of retirement for!

Karaoke Night: What Would Rob Do?

Okay, here's the scene. My not-yet-wife Anna and I were invited to a karaoke bar for a friend's birthday party. Sounds fun, right? Anna and I were coming off an amazing karaoke experience from a few months back where we had the whole bar rocking to Bonnie Tyler's "Total Eclipse of the Heart." I immediately signed us up, thinking we would be the sacrificial icebreakers for the group, hopefully instilling enough confidence in the birthday girl herself to get up and do a song. I scanned the song list looking for another duet for Anna and me to perform and, sure enough, "Total Eclipse" was there. I wanted to try something new, something fun, but something still with '80s flair. Then I saw "Don't You Want Me," a duet by the not-so-seminal British pop group Human League. Perfect.

When I told Anna the song I'd chosen, she gave me a look that said, "Whaah?" I tried to remind her of Human League's strange dreamlike video and sang the first line in my faux English accent, "*You were working as a waitress at a cocktail bar, when I met you . . .*"

She vaguely recalled the song but was unsure. This was not good. Karaoke requires a lot of enthusiasm to get the better of both the song and your nerves. I tried pumping her up.

"We'll be fine!" I said. "Don't worry. The lyrics will be on the monitor!"

We kicked back a couple of pints with our group and watched intently as people from the audience were called up on stage. Finally, the KJ (karaoke jockey) announced our names and, just as I'd hoped, our section began to cheer. Up on the makeshift platform, Anna was a little apprehensive, while I tried to calm things down by humming the tune for her. Suddenly the monitor turned blue, the cheesy Muzak version of the song started up, and the lyrics appeared on the screen, which I belted out with pride: "*You were working as a waitress at a cocktail bar, when I met you. . . .*"

I looked over at Anna, her lines steadily approaching. There was a glint of fear in her eyes. When it came to her part, she tried her best to sing along, but she couldn't keep up because she didn't know the song. I tried to come to her rescue by singing her part in my best female voice, hoping that the crowd would appreciate a more comedic take on the song, but they weren't buying it. This was an L.A. karaoke club, where people with actual talent tested out their performance chops hoping to be "discovered," and they didn't need a *lame-o* guy and his girlfriend wasting their time on stage.

It was clear we were losing the audience. People were averting their eyes. As the song went on, Anna gave up on her lines and shot me an evil look, the one she reserves for when I *really* screw up. I looked to the KJ for help, hoping maybe he'd have mercy on us and cut things short, but he was busy chatting up some Valley girls. We endured all three minutes and fifty-eight seconds of the song onstage. With our heads held low, we returned to our table, our friends embarrassed and speechless. The rest of the party was a bummer, and later that night Anna and I had to "have a talk" about how I shouldn't force her into things without checking with her first.

That is what I'd classify as an abominable karaoke experience.

To figure out how to avoid this kind of scenario in the future, I called Karaoke Mike, a KJ at the Brass Monkey, one of the biggest karaoke bars in L.A. He said picking a song within your range is an excellent place to start. A lot of people think they can nail the high notes in classics like "Sweet Child o' Mine" or "Stairway to Heaven." KJ Mike says these people are delusional, because all the voice lessons in the world won't make you sound anywhere as good as Axl Rose or Robert Plant. He advises picking even-tempo songs that stay within one octave. Personally, I like "Coconut" by Harry Nilsson, or "Ain't No Sunshine" by Bill Withers.

It's also a good idea to stay away from the fast stuff. I've only seen a few guys successfully perform Sir Mix-A-Lot's "Baby Got Back," but have seen far more buckle almost immediately after shouting "I like big butts and I cannot lie . . ." Also steer clear of "rock rap" anthems like R.E.M.'s "It's the End of the World as We Know It," and Billy Joel's "We Didn't Start the Fire," because all you're going to do is mumble a bunch of words and then shout *"JFK, blown away, what else do I have to say!?"*

KJ Mike says slow and simple songs are the best choices. I personally like some of the offerings from the soft rock and easy listening genres. Think of artists like Journey, REO Speedwagon, and Lionel Richie. You also might want to dip your toe into country music with artists like Johnny Cash,

Merle Haggard, or Willie Nelson. These manly melodies are surefire winners with the crowd. There's also Elvis, but I'd stick with the young "Blue Suede Shoes" Elvis, not the fat "Burning Love" Elvis. The King's songs are also short, which brings up another point. Don't pick epic ballads like Don McLean's "American Pie" or Queen's "Bohemian Rhapsody." It's unlikely that anyone in the room (including you) will be enjoying your performance after the fifth minute.

Picking a sing-along is also a smart bet, especially if you have a weak voice. The audience does half the work for you. The number one sing-along choice has to be Neil Diamond's "Sweet Caroline," which is *the* karaoke standard. You don't even have to wait for the music to start. Shout out "Sweet Caroline," and a raucous chorus of "Bum! Bum! Bum!" is sure to follow. Another big sing-along favorite is the B-52s' "Love Shack," though I'm not sure why. If you pick a sing-along, make sure you work the crowd. Blow them kisses, point the microphone out toward them, get up on the speakers and shake your booty. Just don't take off your shirt and do any striptease stuff. Even if you are at the Brass Monkey, nobody wants to see your hairy back.

A different alternative for the melodically challenged is to get a friend or two (or four) up there to sing with you. The more people you have up onstage with you, the more likely one of you will be able to hold a note. And as my wife likes to remind me, if you're doing a duet, it's critical that both of you are on the same page about what song you pick. Draw the line at letting your female partner choose anything from *Grease*. Karaoke is about being goofy, but it's nice to walk home with at least a shred of dignity.

If despite your best efforts to prepare, you find yourself struggling onstage, KJ Mike says any KJ worth his own PA system should come to the aid of singers in trouble. He recalled to me one time when he personally had to bail out Drew Barrymore while she was hurting onstage. When I think back to my brutal karaoke experience, I wish KJ Mike had been there for us, or even just for Anna, because it's not easy singing both parts of a duet by yourself.

One final thought on karaoke night. Let's say you picked a good song early on in the night, like a sing-along, or you scored yourself some brownie points with a nice slow-paced duet with your girlfriend. Your friends might demand an encore. Now it's time for the rock anthem. Def Leppard's "Pour Some Sugar on Me" is a great choice, but the king of karaoke rock anthems is without a doubt Bon Jovi's "Livin' on a Prayer." This song brings together all the elements of a great karaoke song: it's a sing-along, it sounds great sung with a lot of people onstage, and lyrically it's not too tough. Well, all right, there are *some* high notes in there, but people get so pumped up, so carried away by the nostalgia, that you can pretty much get away with screaming along with the rest of the bar. And when that happens, no one will remember how awful you sounded.

Giving a Wedding Toast: What Would Rob Do?

Everyone likes a funny guy. Whether you're throwing out wisecracks while hanging out with your friends or have an audience roaring at the hilarious toast you're giving at a formal event, having strong comedic skills will definitely make you the life of the party.

Unfortunately, not everyone is good at telling jokes. My problem isn't my delivery so much as my memory. I can only think of two jokes off the top of my head.

"What did the bartender say to the sandwich? 'We don't serve food here.'"

And: "What did the zero say to the eight? 'Nice belt.'"

Feel free to use those whenever you want to crack up a fourth grader.

As Steve Martin once said, "Comedy is the art of making people laugh without making them puke." And that maxim has never been truer than when giving a toast at a wedding. According to TheKnot.com, wedding toasts are best when they are "light, fun, and most of all short." This last sentiment is heartily endorsed by Randy and Jason Sklar. They're twin brothers who perform standup comedy, often with material related to sports. I met them in L.A., and we wound up doing sport stories for NPR together on jousting, kickball, and professional grilled-cheese eating (yes, that's technically considered a sport).

Randy and Jason say most people would be well served by taking their toasts and cutting them in half. Long, rambling speeches may be enjoyable for the couple, but they're torture for everyone else in the room. This is especially true with the maid of honor speech, which is sometimes so overly sentimental that you're left poking at your salad while trying to avert your eyes from the grown woman sobbing into a microphone.

Fortunately for guys, our speeches aren't expected to move anyone to tears, though if you can get someone to snort their drink out their nose, that's considered a success. People expect guys to give funny speeches that gently "roast" the couple, but not ones that flambé them. TheKnot.com suggests giving your speech the grandmother test. If you can't say a joke in front of your Bubbie, it shouldn't be in your wedding speech. That means swearing is out, too. Drop the f-bomb in a speech, and not only will you embarrass the couple, you also just got yourself banned from making any future toasts for friends who might also be attending the wedding. I've seen people get into the most trouble when referring to past relationships. Edit any parts of your speech that start with the phrase "Remember that girl you met . . ." There's a difference between ribbing your friend and socking him in the face.

Randy and Jason Sklar are also strong advocates of taking time to prepare your speech. While their humor onstage may appear to be spontaneous, in reality they spend hours prepping and plotting out jokes. Comedy is about timing, and timing takes practice. I learned this the hard way during my own bar mitzvah. After spending months learning how to chant from the Torah, I neglected to put any effort into the candle-lighting ceremony speech, one of the only parts my guests would actually hear in English. My mother said repeatedly, "You have to come up with some funny little poems when you invite your family up to light candles with you during the reception." *How cheesy*, I thought. I had heard some of those poems. They usually had a singsong quality and went something like this.

> For candle number two
> A really good looking Jew
> Please come forward
> Uncle Andrew.

I decided to wing it on my big day. Big mistake. Here's how my candle speech sounded:

> For candle number two.
> Two people that have known me for a real long time.
> Aunt Susan and Uncle Mark.
> Come up here please.

Umm . . . for candle number three.
Another person who's known me since I was born,
My grandma. Come up here, Grandma.

It wasn't pretty. You'd think that, having gone through that experience, I would have wised up in time for my sister's wedding ten years later. Not the case; I was charged with saying the prayer over the challah bread and adding a few words. I knew the prayer by heart, but I had taken a few rounds of shots with my sister's friends before the toast. After slurring through the Hebrew, all I could muster was, "Everybody, go eat your blessed bread." Again, not my best moment. Unsurprisingly, TheKnot.com advises easing up on alcoholic consumption before toasts.

Randy and Jason's last piece of advice is to avoid too many inside jokes. It's better to have the whole room laughing rather than just one table. One way to do this is to spread the ribbing around. Talk about the folks on the other side of the aisle, but make sure you start things off with getting the room to throw in a round of applause for the parents or the hosts. It may build up some goodwill before you embarrass their offspring.

As for me, I wound up having one really good wedding toast (sort of). I helped write the maid of honor speech Anna delivered at her friend Jackie's wedding. We practiced her delivery, deftly interspersed humor with sentiment, explained all the inside jokes, and most important, kept it short. In fact, the only thing that went wrong was that some idiot in the audience was laughing way too loud when Anna delivered it. That brings me to my last piece of speech advice. Don't be the only guy in the room hooting and hollering while your wife delivers her punch lines during a wedding toast. It totally gives you away.

Planning a High School Reunion: What Would Rob Do?

My alma mater can be described as an atypical high school. Germantown Friends is a small Quaker school in Northwest Philadelphia filled with liberal kids from nurturing families. Sure, there were jocks, potheads, and nerds, but nobody took cliques too seriously. For the most part we were all, well . . . Friends. My fifth-year reunion was a complete blast. It was exactly the way we used to party together, except we didn't have to hide in the woods to drink. As most of us were recent college grads, we all had a lot of common ground. I enjoyed hearing about everyone's undergrad experiences and what they were doing at their first jobs. I remember thinking nothing had changed.

My tenth-year reunion was a vastly different experience. My classmates hadn't become less friendly or less willing to reminisce about rappelling off the school's roof in gym class, but we'd been in the real world for six years, and questions that had previously been innocuous now took on greater significance. The tenth-year reunion is when we started sizing each other up.

"What have you been doing with yourself all these years? Are you still living at home? Are you kidding, you're not going to get a master's degree?" Coming into the night, I had felt good about where I was, but I was one of the rare ones who *hadn't* switched jobs at all. I felt like a skipping CD as I said, "I'm working at NPR. Yup, *still* at NPR. Yes, I'm still there!"

It turns out the competition at reunions is usually steep. According to John Cullen, the president of Reunion Planning, Inc., in Akron, Ohio, you're not likely to find too many low achievers at high school reunions because the reunions themselves are self-selecting. People don't go if they're not excited about their careers. Cullen told me an even bigger factor is how people look. He's been in the business for over two decades, and according to his surveys, on average only 20 to 35 percent of people attend their reunion. The top reason for not attending? Two words: weight issues. Cullen's predictions were spot-on for my reunion. A little more than a third of our class showed up for our tenth reunion, and the ones who did looked good. Then again, because I brought Anna with me, I was doing my best to not pay too much attention to any of my old flames.

Cullen agreed that bringing your spouse along can be tricky territory. He said this is where you want to have an upfront conversation with them and remind them how much you love them and how much they mean to you and that, above all, no matter what they see, you chose to be with them and no one else. For my reunion, I was definitely in sync with Cullen's philosophy. I took preemptive measures to avoid awkwardness, and ran through "the smooch list" with Anna ahead of time so she wouldn't be caught off guard whenever she met someone I'd locked lips with eons ago. Overall, my ex-sweethearts were very amicable toward Anna. Like I said, my classmates were all pretty cool.

For Anna's tenth-year high school reunion, she took things one step further. She planned the whole thing. She was inspired to spearhead her reunion committee after hearing stories from my father, a longtime reunion planner. Ever since I can remember, Dad has been leading the charge in planning the many reunions of Haverford High School's Class of 1965. Here are his top planning tips:

1. Pick the Friday after Thanksgiving as your reunion date. Your former classmates will most likely be returning home to visit family for the holiday weekend and will probably be free on Friday.

This is the exact night Anna picked, and indeed a considerable number of her classmates were already home for the holiday.

2. Spend time on finding classmates, not on the venue or music. People want to see as many old friends as possible. Nobody cares about where you are.

Anna took this advice and searched out classmates through Facebook, old phone books, and mass e-mails. She even enlisted help from someone who worked in local city government to look up names. In the end she was able to contact about 95 percent of her classmates, and nearly half of them attended.

3. Watch your budget. You should figure out the costs ahead of time, factoring in things such as mailings, food, and entertainment. Then set the ticket prices based on a conservative turnout. If you get more people attending, you can always put more money into the party.

Anna didn't have her classmates pay for tickets ahead of time, so she split the upfront costs of food and space rental with the five other members of the reunion committee. She made back most of her money after splitting proceeds from the donation box.

4. Don't overcomplicate reunion plans. One year, my dad cut out photos from his yearbook to make decorations. The decorations went largely unnoticed, but his yearbook is forever defaced.

Anna kept things simple. She rented out the top floor of a bar and had them put out some simple appetizers on a foldout table.

5. Don't forget the nametags.

Anna forgot this one, but four out of five ain't bad.

Attending Anna's reunion turned out to be a lot of fun for me, and aside from one awkward moment when I met her ex-boyfriend, it was great seeing all the people from her yearbook come to life. Despite my enthusiasm, I kept my small talk in check, made sure not to reveal anything that might embarrass Anna, and was careful not to be too penetrating with my own questions. John Cullen says the biggest faux pas you can make is to be too nosy. We're all trying to look good at reunions, and the polite thing to do is give people the best chance to do that.

Perhaps the best part of reunions is having a second chance at a friendship. That dweeb from science class may have turned out to be a cool guy worth talking to. Also, if you're not already in a relationship, this may be a great time to reconnect with some of the late bloomers of the opposite sex. The morning after Anna's reunion, we went out to breakfast with a bunch of her old classmates, and I was treated to two hours of nonstop gossip about who was making out with whom the night before. No matter now old we get, it seems some things never change.

Leaving a Good Voicemail Message: What Would Rob Do?

Consider for a moment the true story of a man—let's call him Greg. Greg was attempting to win over the heart of my friend's mother, a recent divorcée. There is little anybody remembers about poor Greg except the infamous voicemail message he left, which sounded something like this:

Hello this is Greg, I just wanted to call and say . . . um . . .
er . . . um . . . G-d damn. Oh no! &$%#! *Click*.

Greg was about as smooth as Mike, the Jon Favreau character in *Swingers* who couldn't stop himself from leaving
a succession of long, rambling messages on the answering
machine of a girl he'd met a few hours earlier. If there's anything to take away from that film and poor Greg, it's that having lame voicemail skills is a surefire way to kill any potential
relationship.

My father, who's been in sales for more than half his life,
told me the message someone leaves you can say a lot about
them. He can often size someone up based on how well they
speak over the phone. "Rambling is the kiss of death in business," he likes to tell me. People want to know the essentials—
your name, why you're calling, and when and where they can
get back to you. The faster you get that information to them,
the better.

How do you leave someone a great professional message?
Dad has three basic rules:

1. Sound friendly, especially if the person you're calling
   doesn't know you. A warm, friendly voice will make the
   person feel comfortable calling you back.
2. Try to encourage the person to call you back by telling
   them you have something to tell them that they're going
   to want to hear. He likes to say, "I have good news for you
   about such and such a thing."
3. Be clear about how to get back in touch. Leave your
   name and number more than once and when you can be
   reached.

Since hearing Dad's ideas, I've been thinking about recrafting my standard voicemail message to something like:

Hello, this is Rob Sachs. I'm at 555-WWRD. I have great news for you about NPR! That's 555-WWRD. I'm here all week, call anytime. Look forward to hearing from you soon.

Then again, perhaps people might appreciate a slightly softer sell.

When you're not leaving a professional message, there are plenty of ways to annoy your friends and family. I've heard people ask rhetorical questions in their messages, such as, "How are you doing? Are you going to the party tonight?" It's weird because you're not really going to get an answer until they call back. Save your questions for the actual conversation. Also, try to avoid using your voicemail messages as a substitute for the real conversation itself. I don't care who you are, if your last name is not Letterman or O'Brien, you have no business doing a five-minute monologue on someone's voicemail.

If you're still nervous about leaving someone a message— like if you're calling about a job interview, or you think the girl you're dialing is "the one" and you don't want to screw it up—you could try something I learned from NPR's Carl Kasell. Kasell is the king of leaving voicemail messages. To make sure he gets all his points across, Kasell jots down notes before he makes the call. This makes a lot of sense, because taking notes not only reminds him of what to say, but also keeps him from getting tripped up like poor old Greg.

Lastly, remember your diction when you speak. Avoid mumbling and overusing verbal tics such as "um," "like," "uh," and "you know." These tics not only make you sound less intelligent, they might distract the person from your actual message.

Now let's discuss the outgoing message. This is the recording people hear when you don't pick up the phone. I've always admired the outgoing message of Dylan McKay on *Beverly Hills 90210* (the original series, obviously): "It's Dylan, you know the drill." Inspired by his laconic style (let's face it, Luke Perry is inspirational in many ways), I've whittled down my own outgoing message to just eight words: "You've reached Rob's cell. Please leave a message." It's so short that the beep comes before the person has time to think about hanging up instead of leaving a message. I've shaved off all the superfluous phrases like "I can't come to the phone," "thanks for the call," and the most excessive one of all, "leave a message at the sound of the beep."

If you're one of those people who want to use their outgoing message as a mode of self-expression, have you considered having a pro record a custom message for you? This is exactly what Carl Kasell does for winning contestants of the NPR quiz show *Wait Wait . . . Don't Tell Me*. He winds up recording about twelve messages a week. That's more than five thousand messages since the show began. Here's an example:

> Wait, wait . . . don't hang up. Cheryl can't come to the phone right now. But if you leave a message she'll call you back after she finishes listening to her favorite NPR podcast and completes her daily crossword puzzle.

I'm not so sure I want to leave Cheryl a message, but having a public radio celebrity handle your outgoing message is pretty cool—ahem—unique. If I could get anyone to record my greeting, it would be Sally Struthers reprising her role as spokesperson for the Christian Children's Fund, and it would sound like this:

> Hi, I'm Sally Struthers, and for just the cost of this phone call, you can leave Rob Sachs a message. Rob finds it very sad when he sees people call and just hang up. So do your part to cheer this guy up and please leave him a message. The voicemail is standing by. *Beep*!

Using guilt tactics to persuade people to leave a message seems more necessary than ever these days. With the rise in texting, e-mailing, and instant messaging, it often takes much longer to leave someone a voicemail and wait for them to call you back. And how annoying is it to find the time to check your own voicemail messages? On many phones you can now look at a missed-calls log to see who you need to call back.

My friend Canaan's voicemail epitomizes this notion that voicemail is too slow and cumbersome in today's technology-driven society. His message is, "Don't leave a message because I don't check my voicemail. Just text or e-mail me." It's slightly off-putting, but at least it's honest. It reminds me of a homeless man I saw once, holding up a sign that said, "I'm not going to lie to you, I need the money for beer."

By the time my daughter starts using the phone, perhaps voicemails will be as obsolete as my vast collection of cassette tapes. In the meantime, it's probably a good idea to put some thought into what you're going to say *before* the message starts recording. Oh, did I mention that if anyone is looking for a public radio personality to record their outgoing message for them, I'm available?

Talking through Cyberspace: What Would Rob Do?

According to the 2004 Nielsen NetRatings, nearly three fourths of all Americans have access to the Internet. Many people feel empowered to say whatever they want online, but there are plenty of codes of conduct for cyber behavior. Breaking them has real-life consequences.

Being born in the 1970s, I'm part of the last generation to grow up in an age before computers. In high school, I didn't have my own Facebook page or Twitter account. I didn't instant-message my friends from class. I didn't even have an e-mail account. All we had was the telephone, which, as a teenage boy, I didn't use much, except to make plans. Letters were another story. With pen in hand, I wrote dozens of them, crafting my words and using little doodles, underlining, cursive, and script writing to convey deeper meanings. I had this misguided idea that my fleeting summer romances from various teen tours could survive vast geographical distances. In return, my female pen pals would send back pages filled with cute little hearts, dotted "I's," or that playful "bubble" handwriting that only girls know how to write in.

Then came e-mail, which trapped my words in the stoic and unforgiving font of Times New Roman. Sure, I could use **boldface**, *italics*, ALL CAPS, and later emoticons ☺, but those never expressed my feelings with the same precision as my own pen. There was so much more room for my words to be misinterpreted. It's no coincidence that those "Let's see if we can date beyond the summer" romances weren't even making it to the customary Thanksgiving reunion. Now things were over by Columbus Day.

My problems with e-mail followed me into my professional life. Somehow I developed this odd form of humor where if somebody e-mails me something really smart, I like to "fake one-up them" as a way of pointing out, "Hey, that was really smart and I'm actually kind of dumb." For instance, somebody might say, "Man, that Dali painting was so metaphysical it blew my mind." I'd reply, "Yeah, kind of like how that Olivia Newton-John song is totally physical." Now, if I had said this out loud in a sarcastic tone, they'd know I was joking. But with no visual or aural cues, you might think (a) I'm making fun of you for trying to sound too smart, or (b) I'm a complete imbecile. Then I'd have to explain how I was trying to be ironic, which is always an awkward endeavor. You'd think I would have learned my lesson through one gaffe, but the rapid-fire nature of e-mail lends itself all too well to repeating the mistake of sending something stupid. I wish someone over at Microsoft could develop software for "foot-in-the-mouth check" that would automatically scan your e-mails for potentially boneheaded lines.

To get more perspective on how to emote online, I called up gadget blogger Joel Johnson. He agreed that sarcasm doesn't translate very well online, especially if the person receiving your e-mail doesn't know you. Does that mean I have to give up my dry wit when corresponding in cyberspace? Johnson suggests I type "Ha! Ha! Ha!" the next time I drop one of my oh-so-witty comedic nuggets. It's the equivalent of adding your own laugh track to your e-mails. (Come to think of it, it wouldn't be such a bad idea if you could embed a little sound file of your favorite guffaw.) Johnson reminded me about emoticons, but those smiley faces are about as cool as a pair of acid-washed jeans decorated with press-on rhinestones. What if instead of emoticons you could insert actual pictures of yourself displaying the appropriate facial expression? I would call mine "Robicons."

Johnson said the best approach may be to simply leave your top-shelf humor for your face-to-face conversations and develop a less hilarious alter ego for your e-mail correspondence.

The one place where you might have better luck telling a joke online is over an instant-messaging (IM) program. Unlike e-mail, the conversation happens in real time, so you have the benefit of knowing right away if someone misunderstood something. Despite that advantage, instant messaging feels too invasive to me. Whenever you start most IM applications, a buddy list pops up to tell which of your friends are online with you. It's kind of like logging into an online cocktail party, except everyone can talk to you at once.

Furthermore, there's no great way to say goodbye on IM. At a cocktail party you can excuse yourself from a conversation by saying you've got to go to the bathroom, or that you need to get another drink. Your spouse could come grab you after you give them the "rescue me" signal. Online, there are no good life-preserver options. You could say that you've got to go, but if you stay online, they'll know you're still there because it says so right on their buddy list. You can use the "away from your computer" option, but what if you happen to IM with someone else who ends up simultaneously IMing the person you told you were leaving? (And yes, this is plausible.) They'll know you were lying.

I was ready to give up IMing altogether until Johnson set me straight. He told me the cocktail party analogy isn't exactly the right way to consider it. "Think of it more like a long extended correspondence," he said. People need to accept that you're never away, they're never away, nobody ever is really anywhere. "You should feel free to float in and out of conversations online with no social penalties." Maybe he's right. I'm still not comfortable always being available to people for a chat whenever

I'm online. To this, Johnson said it's not considered rude if you don't reply when somebody sends you an IM. Something tells me I'd still feel guilty in that situation, but I'm learning.

Yet just when I've gotten the hang of one form of online communication, another one pops up. In the late 2000s, the new craze became social networking sites like Facebook and MySpace. (As of this writing, Facebook is now considered old-fashioned in the wake of Twitter, a social networking site that allows users to post up to 140 characters known as "tweets" that provide constant updates on where you are, what you're doing, and so on.) These are great places to connect with your friends both past and present, and where you can present who you are to the rest of the world. There are definite benefits to being able to connect with a large group of acquaintances in a simple way, and it's especially effective for bands, comedians, and other entertainers who are trying to reach the largest audience possible.

My problem is that I act differently toward different people in real life, yet on a social Web site there's no option for multiple personalities (at least not that I know of . . . Silicon Valley, are you listening?). I'm more reserved and polite with my parents' friends than I am with my high school pals, and I have even stricter boundaries for my professional relationships. With Facebook, every part of you is out there for everyone to see. It may be fun to show your pals photos from the previous night's bar crawl, but do you really want your boss and your mother seeing those pictures you posted online of yourself getting drunk? And yes, there are privacy settings, but after a while it gets to be too hard to remember who is authorized to view what. Another problem is that you can rack up so many friends on these sites that it becomes rather impersonal, and you actually forget who is on the other end reading all the stuff you post and checking out all your pictures and home videos.

Johnson completely agrees. He says you have to be really careful about who you choose to include on these sites, and recommends either creating a closed site for just your closest friends where you can be wacky and crazy, or being on your best behavior on a site that includes a large number of people or has open access to anyone on the Web. It's that gray area in the middle that gets people in trouble. I personally think it's a good idea to keep it clean and leave most of my personal stuff offline. When you work in the media, you know all too well how easy it might be to get burned from an errant post.

There is another issue to be aware of with these social Web sites. Sometimes your friendship with someone goes through a rough patch. When things have soured, you may not want this person to be privy to all the details of your life. You can always remove people from your friends list (or "de-friend" them), but isn't that like slamming the door in someone's face? Again I turned to Joel Johnson, who said sometimes people get too hung up over having an alter ego online and get caught up in believing the fantasy that they have hundreds of close "friends." He says if there's a person you no longer can handle reading whatever you post online (as innocuous as it may be), then you have a larger problem with that person that your real-life self needs to deal with. I agree, you can't hide online forever. Maybe it's time to get out some stationery and write them a note about how you feel.

It's *Ponch*! Meeting a Celebrity: What Would Rob Do?

Growing up in the suburbs of Philadelphia, I didn't encounter many celebrities. I thought it was neat that I went to elementary school with the local news anchorman Larry Kane's daughter. It was a big deal when we got to visit the set of the newscast, but Mr. Kane was just another dad in the neighborhood.

When I was thirteen I had my first real celebrity experience. I came face to face with my idol Charles Barkley, who at that time was playing power forward for the 76ers. I had a life-size poster of Sir Charles prominently hanging up in my bedroom. Each night I would stare at his big smile and his awkwardly shortened legs, which had been compressed in the photo so his six-foot-six frame would fit onto a six-foot poster. Oddly enough, my encounter with him happened when my parents took me to a Phillies game. The guy sitting next to us was listening to the action on a handheld radio, so in between pitches I could hear the late legendary announcer Harry Kalas calling balls and strikes. At one point he noted that Barkley was in attendance. I almost jumped out of my seat. I was scanning the stands when someone behind me yelled that he was sitting about ten rows in front of us. I could feel my gut clench from nervous excitement. My mother reached into her purse and pulled out a pen. "Go ahead," my parents said. Armed with my All-Star Ballot, I set off to get his autograph.

After the radio announcement, a few other fans surrounded Barkley and a security guard was busy shooing people away. As I got closer, I could see he was there with his own kids just trying to enjoy the game. Undeterred, I continued working my way toward him. That's when the security guard caught me. "Okay kid, move along," he said, trying to prevent me from getting any closer. I looked at my idol in desperation but it didn't seem like he was paying attention to what was happening to me. I was about to leave when he looked back and said, "No, he's okay," and waved the guard off. I held out the ballot and feebly asked him for his autograph. He smiled, signed it, and then handed it back to me. I floated back to my seat. When we got home, my mother paper-clipped the autograph to my poster. It stayed there for years (or at least until Barkley got traded to the Phoenix Suns).

Barkley was the only celebrity I met as a kid, but as an adult it's been a different story. Working at NPR has allowed me to meet Bono, Bill Clinton, Rod Stewart, Steve Carell, Glenn Close, Toni Morrison, and many others. Every time I meet one of these people, I get that same little lightning bolt up my spine—not necessarily because I'm a huge fan, but just because I'm excited by the feat of meeting that celebrity.

Take my encounter with Scarlett Johansson during a Beverly Hills press junket for *Girl with a Pearl Earring*. I was helping produce a story with my colleague David Kestenbaum about press junkets and what happens behind the scenes. In the course of Kestenbaum's reporting, he revealed how camera crews camp out in a hotel for a day to get five minutes for their host to talk with the celebrity. The host for whatever broadcast entity gets to show off to their audience that they've met a celebrity and asks the oh-so-prying question "I know this is unrelated, but what's your favorite fast food?" If all goes well, the two will share a laugh together and the host of the show can bask in some of the shine beaming off the celebrity. Studios are more than happy to accommodate reporters, even offering them free lunches, because in turn they get priceless free publicity.

When Kestenbaum and I finally got our turn to talk to Johansson, I couldn't help but be excited. David asked her how she felt about a full day of answering reporters' questions. She freely admitted it was work and often unpleasant. My role that day was to hold the microphones, though David did permit me to ask one question. I asked her what it was like for her to have a twin brother whose life was taking such a different path from hers. She said something about it being nice to have a supportive family. Upon leaving, I was still excited at having added Scarlett Johansson to the list of famous people I'd met, but I also felt a little sadness because, just like meeting Charles Barkley, it was unlikely she was going to remember me. Let's be honest. I didn't "meet" Scarlett Johansson; I just briefly encountered her. What does that make me to her? Nothing, really.

I was down on the whole idea of "meeting" celebrities for a while after that. Even though I was a huge fan of *Da Ali G Show* on HBO, I didn't even get up from my desk when Sacha Baron Cohen came to NPR. I had come to the sad realization that I had nothing to say to celebrities. It seemed all I could really do was shower them with compliments. I felt like this character Chris Farley played on *Saturday Night Live* who, upon interviewing celebrities, would just recall their various achievements, then finish every sentence with an emphatic "That was awesome."

The fact that I was not getting excited about celebrities was actually something that fit well with living in Los Angeles. I learned that it was sort of an unspoken rule that you should act completely unfazed by a celebrity sighting. It's like saying you're too cool to care, or that you totally get that they don't want to be disturbed either. The proper thing to do when you spot a celebrity is to try to act as aloof as they do. I got good at treating celebrities the same way I treat women with excessive facial hair—averting my eyes, putting down my head, and trying to pretend I had never seen them in the first place.

Then one day, when I was sitting in the airport on my way home from covering a story in Reno, I saw him. I knew from the second I gazed upon that thick black hair, round smiling face, and everlasting twinkle in his eye, that it was Erik Estrada, aka Officer Frank Poncherello from the TV show *CHiPs*, my second all-time favorite show growing up—behind, of course, *The Dukes of Hazzard*. I instantly got a knot in my stomach and was overcome with excitement.

There I was, a mere six feet away from him, frozen to my seat, trying hard to look away, as I had done with so many other celebs. But my mind was racing. I remembered all those years of playing with my Ponch action figure, and the countless hours I spent pretending that my red banana-seat Schwinn was actually a motorcycle that I used to patrol Southern California's highways. A few other people noticed him too, but instead of ignoring him, they swarmed on him with pens for autographs and cameras out for pictures. They were breaking the rule! Later, on the plane, I realized I was completely jealous of those people who got to meet him. He seemed genuinely happy to interact with them. He had been smiling, joking, and playing along. How could I have let that opportunity pass me by? It was Erik *freaking* Estrada—one of my all-time favorite guys!

In this case, having my own podcast turned out to be a very cool thing. When I got back home, I decided I needed to know (as a journalist, of course) whether Estrada is annoyed when people approach him and would appreciate the gesture of being left alone. Lucky for me, Estrada was doing publicity for the release of a *CHiPs* DVD and was happy to do a phone interview. Waiting on hold while his publicist connected us, I could barely contain myself. Then Officer Poncherello—um, I mean Erik Estrada—came on the line. This was far better than just running into him in a crowded airport.

When I inquired if it would have been okay if I had talked to him that day in the airport, he was almost stunned that I asked the question. Having been a celebrity for over thirty years, he realizes what a big deal it is for a fan to meet him. He said it takes "less than twenty seconds to sign an autograph, give a hug, or take a picture with someone," but that twenty seconds can make someone's entire day (or month, or year, or life . . . but I digress).

What a cool guy! I still wondered about other celebrities, though. Was this protocol that I was adhering to a little silly? Estrada was adamant that "if you're going to be on television, if you're going to be in movies, if you're going to be in magazines, and you're going to be doing that for an income and that's your livelihood, you've got to expect people to come up to you and say something to you or get in your space and you can't be pissed off about it." If it bothers a celebrity, Estrada thinks they should "get in a different line of work."

I realized that I needed to think about the whole thing a little differently. Perhaps part of a celebrity's job is to be there for us fans when we spot them in person. Taking pictures in public is part of what they signed up for by being famous. Estrada actually considers himself "75 percent public domain," and thinks people "have the right to come up . . . and say hi." If he wants peace and quiet, he stays home.

I think that is the factor I was overlooking. Most celebrities have the power and money to have all the privacy and seclusion they want (except when paparazzi fly over their Malibu estates to ruin their weddings). They could stay home, but chances are if you see a celebrity in Starbucks, they might actually *want* to be noticed.

I once produced a story on poker playing in Los Angeles, and visited a casino frequented by Ben Affleck. One of the regulars told us that Affleck always used to wear hats and dark shades and pretend he just wanted to blend in. But when his disguise worked so well that nobody recognized him, he toned down his camouflage. That's not to say all celebrities are ego freaks. Some, like Estrada, genuinely need to be out in public from time to time, but they take being stopped by fans in stride.

I knew that meeting Erik Estrada would have made my day, but I wanted to know if there was anything I could have said as a fan that would have made his day. His reply? He loves to get genuine compliments, such as when someone tells him they became a cop because of his role on *ChiPs*. There's a difference between uncontrollable genuflecting and giving a sincere compliment. Estrada says if you can do the latter, you'll never have to feel bad about basking in someone else's glow.

American in London? What Would Rob Do?

According to London's official Web site, nearly two and a half million Americans travel to that city each year, contributing over $1.5 billion to its economy. We're London's biggest tourist block, so you'd think that when Londoners see Americans, they'd leap at the chance to make sure we feel welcome. Unfortunately, that's not the case. Far too many Londoners harbor a healthy disdain for us Yankees. Yet we keep coming back, pouring our hard-earned cash into their coffers. Now, before I tell you what to watch out for as an American in London, allow me to explain how I wound up there.

Of the many skills I possess, learning foreign languages is not one of them. In high school French class I struggled to keep up, and almost dropped out the year we had to read the works of French existential philosopher Jean-Paul Sartre without translation. Thinking about abstract philosophical ideas in a language I only vaguely understood was too much for me. I'm convinced I passed the class only because my older brother, Mike, had already taken that course and paved the way for extremely low expectations. Thanks, Mike!

In college, I fulfilled the language requirement by taking Introductory Spanish. This worked out fine until I wanted to study abroad in my junior year and found out that most programs required language immersions. I decided to immerse myself in English, and applied for the study-abroad program in London. I'd been to London once before, and had gotten a kick out of seeing the Crown Jewels of England, catching the musical *Oliver* at the Palladium, and narrowly missing getting run over by a car because I forgot to look right before crossing the street. With such fond memories, why not go back for a whole semester?

During my study abroad in London, I noticed the British were always whispering things under their breath and telling each other inside jokes that made no sense to me. It seemed a bit—well, snobbish. I realized that in some cases, they were actually talking about me. For a slew of reasons, I was sticking out like some daft bloke. In order for you to know what you may be up against, here's a list of the ten things that Londoners hate most about us American tourists:

1. We wear white tube socks with shorts. What's wrong with tube socks, you might ask? I wear them all the time. They're great with sneakers (or "trainers," as they call them). I think their dark socks look stupid with sneakers.
2. We wear baseball hats. They think it's tacky. British style is all about modesty, understatement, and quiet elegance, which on the whole I can appreciate. I draw the line at my freedom to don my Phillies cap. If caps are tacky, wearing a soccer jersey that's an advertisement for the company that sponsors the team is tackier.

3. Speaking of soccer, they don't like that we use the word "soccer" to describe what they refer to as "football." Any Brit will be happy to tell you that Americans have bastardized the word "football" as well. "We don't know the meaning of the word 'football,'" my English friend Andrew says. We also apparently don't know that if there's a "football" match playing in a pub, we have to use our "inside" voices. Which leads me to . . .

4. They hate that we're loud. Living in London is like living in a library. British people are not afraid to shush you. I felt like I was constantly being told to pipe down, especially on the Tube (their subway system). Oh, I'm sorry, where does it say I can't laugh out loud at a joke in public?

5. They hate it when we don't take the time to learn the intricacies of their massive public transportation system, or when we can't figure out the exchange rate. If you really want to tick off a Londoner, stand on the left side of an escalator (this is the side reserved for people moving) while staring at a map. That pain in your back is the daggers being shot out of the eyes of the people behind you.

6. They obsess over the royal family but take offense when asked if they actually know a royal. And don't ask if everything is near Buckingham Palace, because whatever you're looking for probably isn't.

7. They don't like it when we order American beer in a pub. Andrew admitted that Brits are "total beer snobs." Now, you may like the cold crisp taste of a Budweiser, but order it and you'll get disdainful looks from the whole bar. They want you to try their special hand-pulled beer that has a name like Warm Murky Ale. Pumped from

beneath the bar, it'll probably taste like funky B.O. Totally gross.

8. They don't like American breakfasts. It's nearly impossible to find pancakes in London. The International House of Pancakes doesn't even have an outpost there. They also don't understand the concept of steak and eggs for breakfast, so don't order that unless you want to be snorted at.

9. They hate tourists who travel in packs of twenty and are overweight. Quoting my friend Andrew directly, Londoners are tired of seeing "garrisons of fat Americans."

10. They hate it when we imitate their accents and especially when we call their colloquialisms "quaint." This is the biggest sin of all, and one I admit I am guilty of. I have one very bad Cockney accent in my repertoire, and it never goes over well when I use it in front of a Brit. Andrew's skin crawls whenever he hears Americans speaking this way, but my nephew Oliver cracks up when I call him *Aw-lee-vuh*. Save your impersonations for your other American friends.

A list of ten things only scratches the surface of what Londoners don't like about us. Hopefully you won't be worrying about this, as you'll be enjoying London's amazing parks, beautiful architecture, theaters, museums, and authentic hole-in-the-wall pubs. If you find the judgmental eyes of Englishmen getting you down, take a train to Scotland or a ferry to Ireland, where the locals will be more than happy to join you in a hearty round of London bashing. Apparently, Londoners are snooty to them too.

6.

Daddy Dilemmas

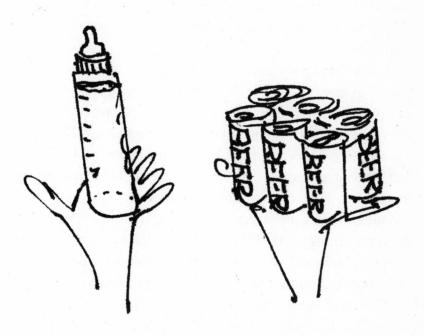

It feels kind of funny to be writing a chapter about fatherhood, because as I'm typing my daughter, Rachel, is a little less than a year old. So don't look for any parenting tips that go beyond the first year, because I haven't gotten there yet. And I don't have much advice about baby boys either, though I hear that "pee-pee teepees," little paper cones you put over a kid's package during diaper changing, are indispensable. That said, the parenting tips in this chapter are mostly gender neutral.

First up, I explore what turned out to be the most difficult part of getting ready for our baby girl: picking out her name. I thought this would be easy until I realized the different criteria a potential name has to clear to be an acceptable candidate. Before Anna and I made our final decision, I talked to an author who's written multiple books on baby naming and found some ways to fast-track the process.

Once we had the name picked out, there was the task of delivering our girl. While it was clear what my wife's role was going to be in the delivery room, my job description was a little more nebulous. I knew she wanted me there for support, but there are many ways to interpret exactly what "support" means. I'll share what worked and what didn't work, as well as advice I got from other dads.

Once you have a baby, you soon discover a whole parallel universe created just for them. They have their own furniture, their own food, and their own musical instruments (these tend to beep a lot). When it comes to music and clothes for babies, some of it is so cutesy you'll want to puke. In this chapter I'll explore ways to dress your kid so he or she looks cool and stylish. I'll also talk to real-life rock-star dad Gavin Rossdale, who helps me figure out how to find kid-appropriate music I'm not ashamed to crank up on my car stereo.

Finally, I look at how fatherhood affects the social lives of dads. My new lifestyle bears little resemblance to my bachelor existence, except for the fact that both involve being awake at all hours of the night. When you're a bachelor, finding your ilk is as easy as heading to a singles bar, but as a dad, sniffing out your own kind is a lot more difficult. Cruising for dads takes more work than looking for the dude with a burp cloth hanging out his back pocket. I take a look at ways to both identify and court "daddy pals."

Diving into fatherhood is not always graceful. At times it can be downright gross. I know I have a lot to learn, but having made it through the first year, I think it's only fair to share some of my triumphs, along with my biggest mistakes. For example, if you're wearing a brand-new shirt, and your kid has eaten a full meal of yogurt, grapes, and pureed peas, try not to jostle her around too much. Consider that lesson one.

Naming Your Baby? What Would Rob Do?

Growing up, I was never shy about giving names to things. I spent practically half my childhood anthropomorphizing every object in my room, usually by sticking a "y" at the end of things. My pillow was "Pillowy," and the curtains, "Curtainsy" (had I been wittier, I could have gone with "Jamie Lee Curtains"). When it came to naming stuffed animals, I could come up with a name on the spot. I had a teddy bear named Fluffy, another named Bear-trice (after my grandmother Beatrice), and my Cabbage Patch Kid (yes, some boys had them) was renamed Ricky. I say "renamed" because he had a stupid name that came on the "birth certificate" in the box. Now I have a father-in-law named Ricky. Coincidence?

Pet names were also a breeze for me. For some reason, I thought Freddy was the ideal name for a goldfish. So I had Freddy, Freddy Jr., Freddy III, and Frederina (she had pretty gills). When I got a fish tank to "pimp out" my college apartment, I named my moor fish Othello, my goldfish Goldie, and my opaquely yellow fish Jaundy. As you can see, I've been confident in my ability to slap a moniker on any animal or inanimate object that I possess.

All this changed when Anna got pregnant. Pets and teddy bears are one thing, but a baby brings a host of memories and visceral reactions to the table. A lot of names I liked were the names of old classmates Anna didn't like, while others didn't go well with "Sachs." I liked Penelope, but Penny Sachs sounded like she was destined to be a pauper. Eventually Anna and I did what millions of couples before us have done, and turned to a baby-naming book. For my podcast I called Linda Rosenkrantz, one of the most well known authors of baby-name books. She's helped write more than a dozen books on the topic, including *Cool Names*, *Beyond Jennifer and Jason*, *Madison and Montana: What to Name Your Baby Now*, and *The Baby Name Bible: The Ultimate Guide by America's Baby-Naming Experts*.

Despite the shelf of books Rosenkrantz has on the market, she first directed me to a free online resource, the Social Security Administration's list of the one thousand most popular names in America. My heart sank when I found a lot of my personal favorites also happened to be the most popular.

Sophia, Olivia, and Emily were all in the top ten in 2007. That killed it for me. I mean, I'm the kind of guy who orders last in a restaurant just so I won't select a dish someone else has picked. There was no way Anna and I would be trendy baby namers. I was determined to at least choose a name beyond the top ten—no, better yet, make that the top fifty to be safe.

Popularity was a factor, but to Rosenkrantz's credit, her books provide a lot of information beyond lists of names. Where they're most helpful is in categorizing certain names by origin and in explaining how some names "sound" to other people. For instance, in *Beyond Jennifer and Jason*, she and coauthor Pamela Redmond Satran lump names together in groups like "Nature Names," "Dutch Names," and "Mythological Names." There's a wide range out there. For instance, if we were looking to honor Anna's New England roots, we could go with Zenobia. Zenobia Sachs? That doesn't have a good ring, does it?

That's the other thing with names. You want them to sound cool coming off your lips. One of my colleagues, NPR's Italy correspondent, Sylvia Poggioli, has about the coolest name around. It's so catchy some guy in Oregon once named a restaurant after her. I wanted to give my daughter something equally memorable, but after I talked to Sylvia about her remarkable name, she confessed it wasn't always easy being Sylvia Poggioli. She got teased a lot as a kid, which is why she places extra emphasis on saying her name correctly. It's worth checking out one of her stories online just to hear her say "*Sill*-vee-*ah* Poh-*joe*-lee!"

Rosenkrantz agreed that giving your kid a name that sounds neat but is hard to spell or pronounce is setting them up for years of ridicule. It's a shame, because I'd grown fond of the name Sasha Sachs. It felt like it had the same flair as Sylvia

Poggioli. Wouldn't it be fun at a dinner party to introduce them to each other? "Sylvia Poggioli! Please-ah meet-ah Sasha Sachs!" Both are names that require exclamation points after you say them. Anna shot "Sasha" down fast. We wanted a name that could be flexible in all types of situations, and Sasha Sachs didn't sound serious enough. In addition, now that there's a Sasha Obama living in the White House, that name will probably become too trendy for me anyway.

Anna and I also considered the "Let's just be out there" route. Inspired by celebrities with crazy kid names like Gwyneth Paltrow and Chris Martin's daughter Apple, or Elle Macpherson's kid Arpad Flynn, I considered picking some random word that popped into my head. It seemed like a good way to ensure she'd be one of a kind. The first word I thought of was "taco." What if we just called our daughter Taco Sachs? Yes, I'm aware that it sounds completely stupid to name someone after a delicious meat-filled Mexican dish, but wait! Close your eyes and say the two names together: Taco Sachs. Cool, right?

Who was I kidding? Naming my kid Taco or Arpad meant never-ending ridicule from my parents—not that a grown man should have to worry about what his mother thinks when naming his own child, but I did mention I have a Jewish mother, right? She would nag me about it until I would just concede and call my daughter by her middle name.

So that's when I thought about choosing a Jewish name. Anna and I had the thrill of visiting Israel while she was pregnant with our daughter. Well, it was a thrill for me. Anna mostly spent her days suppressing nausea as our tour bus bounced through the desert. We did meet a lot of great people with great Israeli names, like our tour guide Yael.

There were a couple of problems we foresaw in giving our daughter a Hebrew name. First was pronunciation. A name like Yael (pronounced *Yah*-el), while common in Israel, could easily be pronounced "Yale" in the United States. I wouldn't want people thinking we had named her after an elite college. That's as tacky as naming your daughter Porsche or Ferrari. Then there was the *chet* problem. *Chet* is the phlegmy letter of the Hebrew alphabet that makes up the "ch" in Chanukah. Instead of a "chuh" like in the word "chain," it's more of a "huh" with a throat loogy thrown into the mix. If we named our daughter Chaya or Charna, we would have to worry about people expectorating all over her while they practiced pronouncing her name correctly.

I asked Rosenkrantz for advice on the *chet* problem, and she said there's really no way of ensuring that people will get it right. "Some people will *chhh* and other people won't," she said. The other reason we shied away from an overtly Jewish name was that we didn't want to pressure our daughter to live up to the religious connotations of her name. For instance, you waltz into a deli with a name like Menorah and order a BLT, they just might refuse to serve you.

Anna and I finally found a happy medium by going biblical. Biblical names are great because they've long since blended into the melting pot of American names while still retaining a Jewish spiciness. The one problem here is that we're not the first Jews to come to this conclusion. I know at least five people each with the names David, Daniel, Jacob, and Benjamin. We liked the name Sarah. Who doesn't like the name Sarah? I mean, she was Abraham's wife, the matriarch of the Jewish people. But between my wife and me, we know at least fifteen Sarahs.

Instead, we went with the name Rachel. We broke a couple of our own rules by choosing it. Anna's first cousin is a Rachel and we both knew a handful of people with that name, but ultimately we chose it anyway. I recognize that a name like Rachel goes against my whole "ordering a different dish from everyone else at the table" rule, but sometimes you really want a steak, and that's exactly what you should get. I love the name we gave our daughter. It's not dorky, not too whimsical, and not too stuck-up. To us it sounded sweet, sporty, smart, and beautiful. It also works well with Sachs. I have to admit, though, there's still a part of me that wants to get crazy with our next child's name. If it's a boy, I'm voting to name him Cole D. Sachs (but that might not work unless we move to a dead-end street).

My Wife Is in Labor! What Would Rob Do?

It's hard to find a more anxiously anticipated life event than the birth of a child. You have months and months of waiting to think about, plot, and plan this event. Yet when that moment arrives, it seems like all the time spent in deep deliberation gets thrown away and you're running on instinct. The one main thought in your head is to get your wife to the hospital before that baby plops out on the floor.

Anna did her best to prepare us. We read books. Lots of books. To be more accurate, *she* read lots of books. When she finished, she handed them off to me with dog-eared pages and highlighted passages. I read as much as I could, not wanting to upset her already volatile hormones. Reading these texts helped me understand there was a whole lot left out of my eleventh-grade sex ed class. I knew I had much to learn (like what the heck is a mucus plug?), but Anna's tomes were usually too dense to get through. Fortunately, I found some titles that spoke more directly to me. I read books like *My Boys Can*

Swim!: The Official Guy's Guide to Pregnancy by Ian Davis, and *The Expectant Father: Facts, Tips and Advice for Dads-to-Be* by Armin A. Brott. Continuing with the theme of books with long titles, I also picked up *The New Dad's Survival Guide: Man-to-Man Advice for First-Time Fathers* by Scott Mactavish. I liked Mactavish's take in particular, since he peppered his text with language I could relate to. For example, this is his advice for witnessing the afterbirth/placenta: "Warning! Do not watch any of this unless you have a great therapist!"

I decided that before Anna started having contractions, I needed to talk to Mactavish to review my game plan. He turned out to be as eloquent on the phone as he was in his book. Here's how he explained the experience of watching his wife in labor. "It brought me around to spirituality. I never really had that in my life until I saw a head pop out of my wife's naughty bits."

As crass as that may sound, there's a lot of truth to that. For me, the birth of my daughter was a strange interplay between being completely grossed out and profoundly moved. It was an exhausting seesawing that lasted one very long night. But before you get to the hospital, you have to plan ahead. Mactavish advised expectant parents to pack a suitcase well in advance of the anticipated delivery date, because from the moment it's "go" time, your mind shuts down and then you're floating on adrenaline. Weeks before our due date, Anna busied herself packing bags with extra clothes, pillows, bathrobes, slippers, a going-home outfit for the baby, toiletries, and a mega bag of Peanut M&M's. I spent that time doing what I do best: combing through my CD collection to put together the perfect mix for the labor experience.

The making of "Labor Mix 2008" required some tough decisions. I considered putting on some upbeat songs to get Anna

fired up about the birthing process. Salt'N Pepa's "Push It" came
to mind, as did the song "Maniac" from the movie *Flashdance*.
Mactavish recommended Survivor's "Eye of the Tiger." After
consulting with Anna, I found out she was hoping for calm and
soothing music. She assured me the act of labor itself would
be sufficient to get her heart pumping. Switching gears, I chose
songs I knew would put her in a good mood. Track one on the
disc was Pachelbel's Canon in D, the music we walked down
the aisle to at our wedding. My thought here was to remind
Anna how I was the nice guy she married, not the sorry dude
who had no clue how to react to the pain she was about to go
through. The rest of the CD followed this theme, with a few
songs from the *Lion King* soundtrack thrown in. It was a blatant
attempt to win some emotional goodwill for the day, and it completely worked.

As far as other mood setters, the hospital has these crazy rules
against incense or candles (something about fire hazards . . .
whatever). I was able to bring in a few other comforts from
home, like a couple of stuffed animals and her favorite pillow.
The last one wound up being a wise decision, because the hospital pillows were rock hard.

While Anna may have been packed and ready a month before
the due date, that doesn't mean I was mentally prepared. Rachel
was scheduled to arrive on February 10, so I diligently made
preparations for that date in the same way I'd plan a vacation.
Except Rachel decided February 10 was too long to wait. Anna
started feeling contractions on the night of February 2. The next
day was Super Bowl Sunday and we had planned a party at our
place, which I then had to cancel. In retrospect, planning a party
when my wife was about to burst may not have been a great idea,
but then again it was nice having a big platter of chips and salsa
waiting for us when we got home.

Getting to the hospital was an ordeal in itself. Anna slowly and calmly waddled out of the house while I ran back and forth loading up the car like a chihuahua on crack. From the moment I started the engine, I suddenly found it very difficult to get myself to step on the brake. Though the hospital was just a five-minute drive away, I managed to run at least three stop signs along the way. At the last one, I almost cut off another car making a turn, and we got flipped the bird by some old lady riding shotgun. Despite the fact that I was clearly the one in the wrong, I let Grandma have it. I laid on my horn for a solid fifteen seconds while following closely behind them. I figured, though, that it was the one time I'd get to justifiably break traffic laws. I was sort of hoping we'd get pulled over so I could get a police escort to the hospital. Alas, that didn't happen.

When we arrived I continued to zip around while Anna hobbled about, stopping every few minutes for a contraction to pass. I stayed downstairs for what seemed like forever to fill out paperwork while she went up to the maternity wing. By the time I made it upstairs, she was already in a hospital gown lying in a bed hooked up to monitors. Anna was in a lot of pain, but relief came not long afterward in the form of an epidural. By that point it was past midnight, and even though she was in active labor, she was able to fall asleep.

But getting some rest wasn't as easy for me. The room had a tiny loveseat for dads-to-be, and I spent the next few hours practicing my Cirque du Soleil moves, contorting my body into various positions in a futile attempt to get some sleep. Eventually morning came and with it a drug called Pitocin, which was used to speed up Anna's contractions. I understood what Mactavish was talking about when he told me labor is "sort of like combat. You're going to have long stretches of complete boredom interspersed with several minutes of abject terror." I felt like a soldier who had been ambushed after being up all night on watch duty.

Somewhere in my head I had imagined that once Anna started the process of pushing the baby out, a team of nurses would jump in and take over. Nothing could've been further from the truth. When the pushing started, the doctor exited the room, leaving me, Anna, and a nurse named Patricia, who turned to me and said, "Grab a leg!"—which, by the way, is exactly what my dad likes to shout at me during Thanksgiving. Before I knew what I was doing, I was right by Anna's side, helping her to count breaths and time her pushes. At first, Anna was a little nervous about the pushing process. I assumed it was the fear of uncontrollable bowels (something those books said might happen). But then after a few tries, something clicked and she got this look in her eyes, not unlike the one David Banner gets right before he morphs into the Incredible Hulk. Anna started pushing like a woman possessed. Back when she was in high school, she had been a star sprinter and hurdler on the track team, and I could see the champion mind-set suddenly resurge in full force. I actually got a little scared.

When the head started to emerge, Patricia finally called the doctor back in, who in turn put Anna's feet in the stirrups, relieving me of my leg-holding duties. Before I knew it, Rachel had arrived. My first reaction was, "Wow, I can't believe something that big was living inside of Anna." My next thought was, "Wow, my life is changed forever." I know everyone always says this, but being there for the birth of my daughter was one of the most terrifying, exhilarating, heartwarming, and nauseating experiences I've ever gone through. (I can only imagine how it felt for Anna.) Perhaps what shocked me the most was when I realized later that this was just day one of being a dad.

Buying Kids' Clothes: What Would Rob Do?

My first foray into buying kids' clothing happened after I became an uncle. It was the early 2000s and I was living in Los Angeles, where the prevailing baby style was "Mini-Grown-Up." Boutiques were selling mini basketball shoes, mini trucker hats, mini wrist bands—anything to make babies look trendy and retro like their parents. While I admit the mini Clash and Ramones T-shirts were rad, I didn't go that route.

To find out more about the hottest kiddy labels, I called up the children's clothing boutique Pancia near Venice Beach and spoke to the owner, Giulia Godi. She directed me toward hip labels like Tomat and Samson Martin. Another big trend was ironic T-shirts from brands like Urban Smalls, with sayings on the front like "Nobody puts baby in a corner." Shopping online, I found another snarky shirt that reads "I don't match because daddy dressed me." What could be cuter than putting words into the mouth of someone who hasn't learned how to talk, right?

As an uncle, I didn't quite understand the economics of kids' clothes, since I was only buying a shirt or two a year for my niece and nephews. I would purchase some overpriced shirt, then find out from my sister that it was ruined a week later by a mixture of spitup and strained peas. Now that I'm a dad myself, I know how moronic it is to buy expensive clothes for kids who are starting to eat solid foods. Perhaps the most ridiculous article of kids' clothing I came across when shopping was a cashmere baby sweater. Whoever designed this either (a) doesn't have children themselves, or (b) has a sick and twisted sense of humor.

In my short time being a dad, I've learned that with baby clothes, color is as important as, if not more important than, style.

When Anna and I started getting pink baby clothes as gifts, we scoffed because we didn't want to limit Rachel to girly stuff. Why did everything for a girl have to be pink? Doesn't this send our child the wrong message about gender roles and limitations? We had plans to dress Rachel up in every hue imaginable, that is, until she came out of the womb as bald as Mr. Clean.

It only took about four people calling our daughter a "handsome little boy" before we realized that we needed to dress her in pink *all the time*. I also became a big fan of putting Rachel in dresses no matter what the weather was like outside. It's not that our little girl had masculine features, but at such an early age, hair seems to be the number one gender signifier. When that's out of the equation, you need to give people another kind of clue.

Once we had colors figured out, we then had to learn about practicality. Getting clothes on a baby can at times feel like trying to put a shirt on a live chicken. They squirm, flip, and scream in protest. In the beginning, I used to stick my face in Rachel's face whenever she was crying in an attempt to make her feel bad about being so rude to her father. That was stupid. It just made her cry harder. I've since learned that getting a baby dressed is all about the art of distraction. "Daddy has a ball! Oooh, look! Pay no attention to what mommy is doing with that shirt sleeve." Another thing I discovered about myself as a father is that I have a deep hatred of buttons, especially the teeny-tiny ones they put on little girls' dresses and blouses. Practicality means buying clothes with snaps.

As far as where we shop, Anna and I found Target, Old Navy, and Baby Gap were great for basics like onesies, socks, and T-shirts. Membership in the Sachs Family Hand-Me-Down Club also helps. My sister and cousin have been great in sending us tons of clothes their own children have outgrown. We've learned to accept everything, no matter if the clothes don't fit, aren't our style, or have food stains on them. We don't want to risk offending the giver and have them cut off our supply line.

Perhaps the most difficult clothing purchase we had to make during Rachel's first year was her Halloween costume. At first we didn't think we would buy one because she'd only wear it once and wouldn't remember anyway, right? Once Anna and I thought it through, we conceded that Rachel only gets to be a sweet little infant on Halloween once. By next year she'll be a toddler, and while toddler costumes are still cute, they're not super-mini cute. So we went all out and spent more than we should have on a chicken suit that Rachel totally hated. This, of course, made her look even more adorable. We officially called her costume "The Angry Chicken."

While buying a fancy chicken suit might seem overindulgent, Rachel did end up wearing it several times during the week to various Halloween parties. A splurge every now and then is definitely worth it. I'm guessing, though, my opinion on this might change once Rachel starts picking out her own outfits.

Annoying Kids' Music: What Would Rob Do?

As someone who loves music, I made it clear to Anna that I wanted us to raise Rachel in a house filled with Bono and Bob Marley, and to do our best to minimize Barney and Bozo. So far, we've been doing a good job mixing up the kiddy music with the stuff I like.

Finding this balance isn't always easy. When I was growing up in the early 1980s, there wasn't much kids' music beyond a few ballads by Peter, Paul, and Mary and the tunes I heard on *Sesame Street*. I used to love to sing that song that follows the pinball counting up to twelve, especially when they'd repeat the last two numbers with such gusto. "Eleven, twelve!" My all-time favorite song was a Bert and Ernie ditty called "The National Association of W Lovers." It was on a Muppets album my mom bought, and I used to play it over and over on our record player.

Truth is, the bulk of my music education came from MTV. I lived for videos like Weird Al Yankovic's spoof of Michael's Jackson's "Beat It," aptly called "Eat It," or Twisted Sister's rock anthem, "We're Not Gonna Take It." Lead singer Dee Snider could easily have been a WWE character. Yet MTV couldn't always be counted on for providing kid-friendly content. The Talking Heads' "Burning Down the House," and Billy Joel's video for "Pressure" completely freaked me out. There's a *Poltergeist*-like scene in "Pressure" where a boy gets sucked into a TV that still gives me nightmares.

Around the late 1980s somebody finally realized a buck could be made actually marketing real rock music to kids. And I'm not talking about the Disney *Kids Incorporated* style of kids singing covers of rock songs, but real bands making real music. One of the first big crossover songs was "Istanbul (Not Constantinople)" by They Might Be Giants (which is a cover). After enjoying a brief mainstream radio run, it became a kids' hit when it aired on the show *Tiny Toon Adventures*. Eventually, They Might Be Giants fully capitalized on their new audience and started making albums solely for kids.

I would have missed out completely on the new kiddy music revolution were it not for an internship I did in college on *Kids Corner*, a radio show produced at WXPN in Philadelphia. Hosted by Kathy O'Connell, the show focuses on both music and education. On the music side, it features mainstream acts like Weird Al and They Might Be Giants, as well as folk rock kids' groups like Trout Fishing in America and Tom Chapin. Hearing all these great songs, I realized there was life beyond Barney and all that whiny saccharine children's music that subversively burrows deep into your skull so you're stuck singing it all the time. Perhaps no other group has represented the coming of age of children's music as much as the Wiggles.

Although relatively unknown to adults without tots, in the world of kids' music the Wiggles are international superstars, boasting sales of more than seventeen million DVDs and four million CDs. In 2007, they beat out more well-known stars like Kylie Minogue, Hugh Jackman, and Russell Crowe for the title of Australia's highest-earning entertainers. They grossed in excess of $45 million that year alone. Not bad for a band that had never even charted one Top 100 hit in the United States. I did a story on the group for NPR and spoke with Kathy O'Connell about what makes the Wiggles such a sensation. She explained it's because they have roots as a real rock band. Group members Anthony Field (Blue Wiggle) and Jeff Fatt (Purple Wiggle) were once members of the Cockroaches, a successful Aussie band from the 1980s.

After leaving the band, Field went on to get a degree in early childhood development at Australia's Macquarie University. There he met up with Jeff Page (formerly Yellow Wiggle) and Murray Cook (Red Wiggle). During an interview with the band, Field told me the guys initially created the Wiggles as a way to amuse their friends' kids at birthday parties, but soon demand grew, so they started playing larger and larger venues. "First and foremost we're entertainers, and then we're educators," Field explained. O'Connell agreed that this is the key element to their success. They approach the idea of creating a song by first finding a really catchy hook, and then they weave in the educational stuff, not the other way around.

My nephew Oliver was a huge Wiggles fan for a while. He never made it backstage, but he did get a high five at a concert from Red Wiggle, which was the highlight of the year for him. By the time he was four, Oliver had a complete Wiggles wardrobe—Wiggles socks, Wiggles pajamas, Wiggles shirts, even Wiggles underwear. I asked the group how they felt about making such a strong impression on kids. Red Wiggle (Cook) recounted a strange experience he had once when he saw a little kid at the airport dressed up completely like him. "That was kind of an out-of-body experience," he told me.

I am not completely against playing kids' music for my daughter as long as I can stand listening to it too. The Wiggles pass that test for me, and I hope other bands emerge with the same level of talent. But I wondered what adult rockers play for their kids. For that answer I turned to a bona fide rock-star dad, Gavin Rossdale. He's the former lead singer of the band Bush. Their 1994 album *Sixteen Stone* sold over eight million copies on the strength of hits like "Glycerine" and "Machinehead." And let's not forget, Rossdale's wife is herself a rock star— Gwen Stefani from the band No Doubt. Together Rossdale and Stefani have two sons, Kingston and Zuma. As you might expect, the couple likes to keep their children's musical diet homegrown whenever possible. At three years old, Kingston listens to his parents' records all the time. "Like all kids, he just likes a good tune and a good rhythm and so my whole record [his solo album *Wanderlust*] seems to appeal to him," Rossdale told me.

I asked Rossdale if he was concerned about his kids listening to their parents' songs that contain profane lyrics and/or adult themes. Perhaps he's tempted to change the lyrics if he's singing one to his son? Rossdale was quick to dismiss that idea.

"What, censorship that early on? That would be a terrible path to tread. There will be certain stickier moments when I have to explain certain elements of things, but I'll try and be as evasive and fast as possible," he told me.

When I thought about it, I didn't think my parents had tried to censor my musical tastes either. Maybe if they had, I wouldn't have had to go bed fearing Billy Joel every night. Rossdale feels differently about shielding his son from Bush's racier songs. "It's a weird and wonderful world out there," he said, "[and] the least he needs to worry about is my lyrics." Admittedly, Rossdale's lyrics are tame compared to what you'd find on my Prodigy or Rage Against the Machine albums. I probably wouldn't be psyched to hear my daughter repeat lines she picked up from those records, at least not while she's learning to talk.

I discussed the issue of appropriate music with my NPR colleague and fellow dad Felix Contreras to see what he plays for his kids. Like me, Felix tries to strike a balance by playing bands such as the Wiggles, but also throwing in the occasional Beatles, Rolling Stones, or No Doubt song. I'm also a big fan of albums that bridge the gap between adults and kids. For instance, Bruce Springsteen made an album of Pete Seeger's classic children's folk songs. Indie-rocker Lisa Loeb has reincarnated herself as a kiddy bard, and the Barenaked Ladies, the crazy Canadian band, released an album of kids' tunes called *Snacktime*, which perks up Rachel every time we put it on.

Deep down I know there will come a time when the forces of children's TV will become too great and my daughter will start singing some annoying song she learned on *Dora the Explorer* or *Barney and Friends*, or repeating a jingle from a cheesy commercial. I'm hoping if I give her early exposure to real authentic music, she will also be able to develop an ear for good tunes. Seeing the widening range of quality music out there, I'm optimistic I can actually pull this off.

Having a Life while Being a Dad: What Would Rob Do?

When you're a little kid, making friends is as simple as sharing the toy you happen to be playing with. Your mom plunks you down next to another kid, he seems to like GI Joe as much as you, and bam—you're friends. Once I became a married man, I found myself participating less and less in the standard male bonding activity of drinking and began noticing that it wasn't quite so easy to keep friends. All my pals who were busy chugging Vodka Red Bulls started drifting away. Thank goodness my core group of longtime friends chose to keep hanging around, but even they had to readjust to the fact that my social scene was rapidly changing. I would constantly be encouraging them to bring along a date whenever they hung out with me and Anna so they wouldn't feel like a third wheel.

Once Anna and I had Rachel, nights out became a luxury. Seeing a movie with friends required a week or two of planning, not to mention a good chunk of cash for babysitting. In high school, I only got ten dollars an hour as a caddy lugging around two full oversized golf bags around eighteen holes. Now we're paying a very kind lady five dollars more an hour to sit in our living room while our tot sleeps in her crib? Okay, so this woman does know infant CPR should there be an emergency, but it seems like a better deal for her than for me. Our nights out became few and far between, and after the first six months of fatherhood, my social life was in shambles.

Anna saw her circle of friends change dramatically too, but for the most part it was positive. As a work-at-home mom, she was fortunate to find other new mothers through a local moms' club. It's a great outlet not only for play groups, but also for the weekly "Moms' Night Out" they organize. I was glad to see Anna have some time for herself, but I was also a little jealous. Were there any dads' clubs out there?

After days of searching, I couldn't find an equivalent type of organization. Where I did have some luck was with groups that cater to both parents. One is a Seattle-based program called PEPS, or Program for Early Parenting Support. It's run by Harry Hoffman, a father of two grown kids. Hoffman's first piece of advice for finding new dads was that I should (surprise!) join a parenting support group. He said in 2008 his organization saw a 25 percent increase in male attendance. With more and more dual-income households, hands-on parenting is something dads are taking on in greater numbers. According to the U.S. Census, the number of stay-at-home dads is still relatively minuscule compared to the number of stay-at-home moms, but it steadily rose through the 2000s. Although it's still uncommon for men to become full-blown Mr. Moms, the days of fathers not knowing how to change a diaper are long gone.

While it's good to know other dads are accepting greater and greater responsibility at home, I wasn't keen on joining a support group. I didn't need or want another guy's shoulder to cry on. I just wanted to find a few cool dads I could watch a football game with.

Searching out these new friendships, I've also been mindful to do my best to maintain my connections to my childless friends. I've managed to escape for a night out at a bar here and there, but I often feel like an outsider because I'm usually the only dad in the group. I hesitate to bring up baby stuff because from my experience, guys aren't too interested in hearing about it. Then again, it's such a huge part of my life now that it's awkward having to keep it in the bag all the time.

The few times I've hung out with other dads, it's been great to be able to share this new part of me. The only problem: it's hard to find other new dads. My initial approach was blatant "daddy cruising." I decided to work the jungle gyms, take Rachel for extended stroller rides, and casually bring her out to a supermarket so I could roll up to another guy wheeling his kid in a cart and say, "Hey, what's up?" That didn't go over well. Apparently having a cute kid with you only works when you're trying to attract women, not other dads.

I came to realize that fatherhood doesn't all of a sudden make you stop enjoying all the things you did before you were a dad. It just means you have fewer opportunities to do them. Instead of trying to find dads who were still adapting to their new roles, I decided to scope out cool dudes who also happened to be new dads. I brought in Anna to help "pimp me out." Essentially I have her on the lookout for Johns, Toms, Bens, or whoever is married to her mommy friends, in the hope that one of them will be cool enough to hang with. It's a slow process, but it seems to be working. When we're getting together with another couple, Anna's been great at turning on a football game and then quietly excusing herself and making small talk with the wife so that I can have some one-on-one time to get acquainted with the husband. Sometimes I'll stop and think about how weird this feels. It's almost like dating all over again, except at the end of the night, I'm really only looking for a high five.

To see if this sounded familiar to anyone else, I talked to my brother-in-law, Josh, who has three kids with my sister, Andrea. Josh too found himself "making friends by default," as "they were usually the husbands of Andrea's mom friends." While I'm relieved I'm not the only one making my wife do the hard work of extending my social network, I feel that waiting for other dads to come to me is too passive.

I asked Josh if having a shared dramatic experience could fast-track a friendship, the same way boot camp forges bonds between soldiers. I could "accidentally" forget to put a diaper on Rachel one day when I'm out at the swings and ask a new dad for some help. That would make for some good bonding, right? Josh said that could work, but it would also be pretty stupid. He told me that when you're having daddy time with your kids out in public, you're paying attention to them. It's not a good time to meet other dads. He also questioned whether I really wanted to start a friendship by having someone pity me for my incompetence. He has a point. When I imagine the types of guys I'd like to be friends with, having them see me as the "lovable loser" doesn't seem too appealing.

Both Josh and Harry Hoffman of PEPS agreed that eventually I'll be pulled into a lot more scenarios where friendships will happen naturally. As Rachel gets older and becomes more involved in activities, it'll be a lot easier to meet other parents. One place where Josh has made a lot of other dad friends is at his kids' soccer matches. I've seen these "games," which are scrums of five-year-olds moving en masse after a ball. There's really no coaching to be done from the sidelines, so it's been a good place for Josh to meet people. However, the best place to meet dads, Josh said, is the birthday party circuit.

I couldn't believe I hadn't thought of that! Birthday parties used to be my bread and butter for meeting women. "So how do you know [fill in the name of birthday girl]?" was a far more effective pickup line than "Hey baby, I like that dress." In fact, I first met Anna at a birthday party for our mutual friend Logan (see "Matchmaking? What Would Rob Do" in chapter 2).

As I write this, we're only a month away from Rachel's first birthday party, and Anna has done an amazing job of stacking the guest list with new dads. There will be at least six in attendance, including a few I haven't met yet. I don't want to blow this opportunity. I need to play it cool. I don't want to come off as some desperate guy macking on potential daddy friends at his daughter's birthday party, right? Thank goodness, Josh is planning on coming. I'm making him my wingman for the afternoon.

•

What Would Rob Do . . . Next?

At this point you've read through a good amount of what I did, what I should have done, how I'd do it in the future, and how, if you look like Fabio, you're never underdressed for a party. When I started this project, it didn't seem possible that I'd be able to find enough material for a whole book, yet every time I think I've run fresh out of ideas, something inevitably happens to me and I think, "Oh, here's another one."

By embarking on this quest to conquer my most embarrassing moments, I think I was hoping to unearth the hidden secrets of skating by. But much to the disappointment of my innate laziness, the message kept coming back the same way: "Do your homework, practice, and study to master whatever scenario you're in." Hopefully, my many stories of failing to beat the system have been a clear illustration of that.

In addition, I've learned how each new phase of life presents new challenges to overcome. Every day that I've been a father, I have a greater sense of the vastness of uncharted territory in my life. Little Rachel is just learning to walk, and in no time will be talking. Before I know it, I'll be teaching her how to ride a bike and play basketball with me. There's lots ahead, which means plenty of room to screw things up.

But I also think that one of the best lessons I can teach her is not to have too much pride to ask for help. I always get so annoyed when one of my colleagues at NPR acts all shocked when I admit I don't know the name of somebody they're talking about. It's true, I may not know the name of the energy secretary, but then again most of my colleagues probably can't quote song lyrics from the Flaming Lips. We all need to respect that everyone has a different area of expertise. And even when we do know something, someone else is bound to know just a little more. When you approach things with the humble recognition that there are few human endeavors that haven't been tried before, you'll realize that somewhere out there, someone has information that could make it easier for you.

One of the biggest lessons I've learned through my work is that people love it when you ask them for help. There's no better way to win over friends, colleagues, or family members than to defer to them as experts every once in a while. After three years of podcasting, I'm a lot less reticent about asking for help than I was in the past. I also try to be a little more forgiving of myself when I do screw up. Of course, I still learn a lot of things the hard way, but I'm trying to minimize how often that happens.

What I've come to appreciate the most is how fortunate I am to have had the support of my family as I've dealt with the shame of zits, missteps into dog poop, and my not-so-talented talent show performances. I also feel tremendously lucky to have Anna's love and companionship as we navigate parenthood and life in general. She's a very patient woman, not to mention a world-class clutter buddy.

In the end, gaining a broader perspective is what this book is all about. Recognizing that embarrassing, emasculating, and undeniably regrettable things really do happen to everyone (or at least a notable portion of the population) is not only a good thing, it's downright liberating. It seems to me that if you can't laugh at your own shortcomings—well, then you're missing out on all the fun.

ACKNOWLEDGMENTS

There are many people who have helped grow *What Would Rob Do?* from a little idea into a podcast, and finally a book. First, thanks to Jay Kernis and Eric Nuzum: Jay for listening in on the early pilots and giving me great feedback and Eric for sticking with me for all these years and believing that this idea would translate from the air onto the page. You two are the ones who stayed behind me from the get-go and encouraged me to go for it. Eric also introduced me to my wonderful agent, Jane Dystel, who's been a tenacious advocate for me through every step of the process. Miriam Goderich provided amazing support, everything from looking over my proposal to making countless phone calls on my behalf. Thanks also to Randy and Jason Sklar and Brian Unger for teaching me how to interject humor into journalism, as well as for all the support and advice they offered along the way.

I'd also like to thank all of my public radio colleagues who have guest co-hosted my podcasts: David Kestenbaum, Mike Shuster, Mike Pesca, Andrea Seabrook, Karen Grigsby Bates, Madeleine Brand, Felix Contreras, Alison Bryce, Neda Ulaby, Susan Stamberg, Paul Brown, David Folkenflik, John Ydstie, Steve Inskeep, Ari Shapiro, Lynn Neary, Linda Wertheimer, Luke Burbank, Sylvia Poggioli, Lisa Simeone, Charlie Mayer, Carl Kasell, Linda Holmes, Todd Mundt, and Tamara Keith. They took time out of their schedules to help me out and, in the course of doing so, made me sound much, much better than I ever could have imagined. For that I am grateful.

I would also be remiss not to mention the good folks at NPR Digital Media, including Robert Spier, Wright Bryan, Adam Martin, Trey Graham, Demian Perry, Michael Katzif, and Andy Carvin. And I can't forget the people who've helped my video efforts: John Poole, Christopher Toothman, and Monika Evstatieva. Of course my biggest debt of digital gratitude is to the guys behind the What Would Rob Do? Web site, Alex George and Josh Levie. Thanks for creating a great site and helping me spread the word.

From Wiley I want to acknowledge the great work of my editor, Tom Miller, who believed in a new writer and totally got my jokes (potty humor and all). To Brando Skyhorse: I never met you, Brando, or even talked to you, but you're a great editor and connoisseur of '80s pop culture. I had the great fortune to be put under the watchful eye of the wonderfully talented production editor Rachel Meyers. The number of mistakes she caught was truly humbling. I also want to thank Dan Crissman and Jorge Amaral and all of the other people behind the scenes at Wiley who have been helpful in answering questions and keeping me informed about the whole process.

To my parents, Herbert and Alice Sachs, thank you for your unconditional love and support and for teaching me both how to laugh and how to laugh at myself. To my brother, Michael, and sister, Andrea, thanks for always giving me great advice on everything from dating to diaper changing, and for continuing to look out for your little brother. (And yes, Andrea, you get the credit for coming up with the title.) Thanks also to my brother-in-law, Josh Otto, for being a great illustrator and friend. As long as we're talking about friends, thanks to my oldest buddies, Alex, Brendan, Jeff, Matt, and Vincent, who have witnessed my most moments of greatest indignity and still stick with me. Now that's true friendship.

Most of all I'd like to thank my wife, Anna, and daughter, Rachel. Rachel, you were only a bump in your mom's tummy when I started this project, but now your mother and I have had the privilege of watching your first steps, your first words, and your first boogie woogie at your first rock concert. You've forever changed our lives, and we couldn't be happier. Anna, there's not much else I can say that hasn't already been said in this book except thanks for the countless hours you dedicated to fact-checking, spell-checking, and grammar-checking. You've read and reread and reread every word of this book more times than I could have imagined. Thank you for your honest feedback and for letting me know whenever I crossed the line from entertaining to gross. You are truly my best friend, and five years into marriage, I still pinch myself every morning I wake up and see you lying next to me.

Finally, I'd like to thank all the people who've been following the *What Would Rob Do?* podcast and who continue to support my efforts online, on air, and in print. You guys rock!

INDEX

acting, 145–149
Affleck, Ben, 174
airplane seating, 25–30
Air Supply, 59–61
alcohol
  bottle service, 82
  ordering macho drinks, 83–86
  wedding toasts and, 156
  See also nightclubs
American Association for Nude
  Recreation (AANR), 92
American Idol, 139
American Pet Products
  Manufacturers Association, 9
American tourists in London,
  175–178
America's Best Cleaners, 11–13
Antiques Roadshow (PBS), 94
aphrodisiacs, 52

AsianDating.org, 54
AutoCult.com, 22
autographs, 170–171

baby names, 181–186
bad habits, conquering, 100–102
baking, 50–51, 53
Ballard, Chris, 88–90
Banowetz, Dean, 139–140
barbers, 138–140
Barkley, Charles, 170–171
bars. *See* nightclubs
*Basic Black: Home Training for
  Modern Times* (Bates), 79
basketball, pickup games, 86–90
basketball shot carnival game, 44
Bates, Karen Grigsby, 79
TheBathroomDiaries.com,
  103–104

beaches, nude, 90–93
"beach etiquette" cards, 92–93
beer, 84–86. *See also* alcohol
benzoyl peroxide, 110
betting patterns, 65
Beverly Hills 90210, 163
Beyond Jennifer and Jason, Madison and Montana (Rosenkrantz), 182, 183
blemishes, 106–110
body/personal habits, 98–100
  cleaning clutter, 122–128
  conquering bad habits, 100–102
  finding public restrooms, 102–106
  fitness and weight loss, 130–133
  hair styling, 137–140
  passing gas, 133–137
  protecting voice, 128–130
  remembering names, 114–118
  snoring, 110–113
  toilet clogs, 118–122
  zits, 106–110
bottle service, 82
bouncers, 80–83
Boye, Brian, 109–110
Brass Monkey (Los Angeles), 151
Breathe Ease, 113
Breathe Right, 111
Buffer, Michael, 4, 75–76
buffets, 66–69
business casual dress, 78

California High Patrol (CHiPs), 22
call boxes, in elevators, 20
capsaicin, 71
Captivate Network, 20
carnival games, 41–46
Carnival Undercover (Witter), 43–44
casual dress, 78
CDs
  creating mixes on, 37, 187–188

for hypnosis, 101–102
radar and, 23
  See also music
Celebration, The, 34
celebrities, meeting, 169–175
chicken breasts, cooking, 52
"chick flicks," avoiding, 34–36
childbirth, 186–190
CHiPs (television show), 143–144, 173
cleaning services, 127–128
clothing
  for children, 191–193
  for parties, 77–80
  shoes and dog poop, 17–18
  stains, 10–14
  of tourists, 176
clutter, 122–128
"clutter buddies," 125
coloring, for hair, 139
competitiveness, 63–64
  buffets, 66–69
  catchphrases, 73–77
  eating hot peppers, 69–73
  flea market shopping, 93–96
  nightclubs, 80–83
  nudity, 90–93
  ordering drinks, 83–86
  party clothes, 77–80
  pickup basketball, 86–90
  poker, 64–66
compound stains, 11
concealer, 107–108
Contreras, Felix, 197
Converse, Gordon S., 94
Cook, Murray, 195, 196
cooking, 49–53
costume parties, 78
"courtesy flush," 120
Crossfit Wichita (Wichita Falls, Texas), 131
Crown Plumbing and Heating (Frederick, Maryland), 119

crying, speeding tickets and, 24
Cullen, John, 157–158, 160
cyber behavior, 165–169

dancing, 46–49
D'Aniello, Jacob, 16–18
dating, 32–33, 201–202
    cooking romantic meals, 49–53
    creating music playlists, 36–40
    dancing and, 46–49
    dating services, 53–56
    love songs, 56–61
    movie dates, 34–36
    nightclub admission and, 83
    remembering names and,
        114–115
    winning carnival games, 41–46
Dave's Insanity Sauce, 3, 71, 72
Davidson, Mike, 29
Day to Day (NPR), 2–3
dedicated dumping zones
    (DDZ), 126
defecation
    clogged toilets and, 118–122
    dog poop, 9, 14–18
    See also restrooms
"de-friending," 169
Deutch, Howie, 35, 36
deviated septum, 112
Difford, Chris, 38–40
DiFrancesco, Edith, 19, 20
dog poop, 9, 14–18
Doody Calls, 16–18
DOOR OPEN buttons, in
    elevators, 21
Dukes of Hazzard, The, 143,
    147–149
Duke University, 130–131

Edwards, Bob, 128
eHarmony, 54
elevators, stuck, 18–21
"elevator TV," 20

e-mail, 165–166
emoticons, 165, 166–167
Estrada, Erik, 4, 143–144, 173–175
exercise, 130–133, 148–149

Facebook, 168–169
fatherhood, 180–181
    baby names, 181–186
    buying clothing for children,
        191–193
    childbirth and, 186–190
    cleaning services and, 127–128
    male friendship and, 198–202
    music for children and, 193–198
    obesity risk and, 130–131
Fatt, Jeff, 195
Field, Anthony, 195
"filler foods," 68
Fino, Rocky, 51–52, 53
fitness, 130–133, 148–149
flappers (toilets), 121
flatulence, 133–137
flea markets, 93–96
food
    American tourists in London
        and, 178
    buffets, 66–69
    flatulence and, 135–136
    hot peppers, 69–73
Food Marketing Institute, 70
formal attire, 78
friendship, male, 198–202
Frumin, Steve, 81–82

Garage Specialists, 124
gas, 133–137
GasBGon, 136
Germantown Friends School, 157
Gas-X, 136
Glass, Ira, 128
Golden Plunger Award, 103–104
Gordon, Phil, 65–66
GQ, 12

Great Allentown Fair (Allentown,
    Pennsylvania), 42
Grossan, Murray, 112–113
Grossman, David, 27

hair style, 137–140
Hebrew names, 184–185
Henson-Conant, Deborah, 20–21
high school reunions, 157–160
Hirschkop, David, 3, 71, 72
Hitchcock, Russell, 59–61
Hoffman, Harry, 199, 201
Hoops Nation (Ballard), 88
hot peppers, 69–73
housework, 127–128
humidifiers
    snoring and, 113
    voice protection and, 129
Huza, Sharron, 136
hypnosis, 101–102

IndianMatchmaking.com, 54
indignities, defined, 6–7
INeedMotivation.com, 101
"I Need Motivation" (Premji),
    101–102
instant messaging (IM), 167–168
Internet behavior, 165–169
involuntary tells, 65
irritable bowel syndrome
    (IBS), 134
"Istanbul (Not Constantinople)"
    (They Might Be Giants), 194

JDate.com, 54
"Jewfro," 137
Jewish names, 184–185
Jimenez, Umberto, 22, 24–25
Johansson, Scarlett, 171–172
Johnson, Joel, 166–169
June Fete (Huntingdon Valley,
    Pennsylvania), 41

Kane, Larry, 170
karaoke, 149–153
Karaoke Mike, 151–153
Kasell, Carl, 162, 163
Kestenbaum, David, 72–73, 171
Kids Corner (radio show), 194–195
Knee Defender, 28
TheKnot.com, 154, 156

labor, 186–190
Lanzoni, Fabio, 4, 33, 78–79
Las Vegas, buffets at, 66–69
leg room, in airplanes, 25–30
"Let's get ready to rumble!"
    (Buffer), 75–76
license plates, radar and, 23–24
liquor. *See* alcohol; nightclubs
London, American tourists in,
    175–178
Lorayne, Harry, 117–118
love songs, 56–61

Mactavish, Scott, 187
maid of honor speeches, 154, 156
makeup, 107–108
male friendship, 198–202
Marder, Jonathan, 124–128
marriage, 33
Martin, Steve, 154
Match.com, 54
matchmaking, 53–56
McHone, Bob, 119–121
meals, 49–53
memory devices, for names,
    114–118
Mexican food, 70
MGM, 68
milk bottles carnival game, 45–46
mix tapes, 36–40, 187–188
Modern Drunkard Magazine, 83
Montez, Ron, 46–49
Morning Edition (NPR), 142–143

motherhood
    labor and delivery, 186–190
    obesity risk and, 130–131
    See also fatherhood
mouth guards, 102, 113
movie dates, 34–36
muscle mass, 132–133
music
    for children, 193–198
    creating playlists, 36–40,
        187–188
    dancing and, 46–49
    love songs, 56–61
Muzak, 19–20

names
    for babies, 181–186
    remembering, 114–118
nasal blockage, 112–113
National Institute of Diabetes
    and Digestive and Kidney
    Diseases, 133–134
National Public Radio, 1
    Day to Day, 2–3
    Morning Edition, 142–143
    Wait Wait . . . Don't Tell Me,
        163
    What Would Rob Do?, 1, 3–4,
        6–7, 9
    *See also individual names of NPR
    on-air personalities*
National Toilet Map (Australia),
    103
Nature's Miracle, 18
naturists, 92
*New Dad's Survival Guide: Man-
    to-Man Advice for First-Time
    Fathers, The* (Mactavish), 187
Newsvine.com, 29
Nielsen NetRatings (2004), 165
nightclubs
    gaining admittance, 80–83

    ordering drinks in, 83–86
nudity, 90–93

obesity, 130–133
O'Brien, Glenn, 12
O'Connell, Kathy, 194–196
Old Country Buffet (Las Vegas), 67
opera, 129–130
organization, for clutter, 122–128
Otis, Elisha, 19
Otis North and South America, 19
Otto, Andrea Sachs (sister),
    4–5, 201
Otto, Josh (brother-in-law), 201
outgoing phone messages, 163
Oxy, 108

Page, Jeff, 195
paper clutter, 122–128
parenthood. *See* fatherhood
party clothes, 77–80
PBS, 94
personal habits. *See* body/personal
    habits
*Phil Gordon's Little Green Book:
    Lessons and Teachings in
    No Limit Texas Hold'em*
    (Gordon), 65
physical fitness, 130–133,
    148–149
pickup basketball, 86–90
"pierce and drain" technique, 109
pillar procedure, 113
pimples, 106–110
plungers, 122
podcasts, 3
Poggioli, Sylvia, 193
poker, 64–66
Poker: The Real Deal (Gordon), 65
Pollack, Sydney, 36
power washers, 17
Premji, Frederic, 101–102

professional dog poop removers, 16

Program for Early Parenting Support (PEPS), 199, 201

public image, 142–145

  acting, 145–149

  of American tourists in London, 175–178

  high school reunions, 157–160

  Internet behavior, 165–169

  karaoke, 149–153

  meeting celebrities, 169–175

  voicemail messages, 160–164

  wedding toasts, 153–156

public restrooms, 102–106

public transportation (London), 177

public urination, 105–106

"Pulling Mussels (From the Shell)" (Squeeze), 38–40

Racin, Mary Ann, 103–104

radar detectors, 23

red wine stains, 12

relaxation therapy, 101–102

resistance training, 132–133

restrooms

  finding public restrooms, 102–106

  toilet clogs, 118–122

Reunion Planning, Inc. (Akron, Ohio), 157–158

reunions, 157–160

Rich, Frank Kelly, 83–85

Rikon, Shoshanna, 55–56

Rippetoe, Mark, 131–133

romantic meals, 49–53

Rose Bowl Flea Market (Pasadena, California), 95–96

Rosenkrantz, Linda, 182–185

Rossdale, Gavin, 196–197

rowing machines, 132

royalty, 177

Russell, Graham, 59–61

Sachs, Anna (wife), 5, 55, 186–190

  on high school reunion planning, 158–160

  karaoke incident and, 149–151

Sachs, Mike (brother), 4–5, 24

Sachs, Rachel (daughter), 5, 204

  birth of, 186–190

  naming of, 181–186

  See also fatherhood

Sachs, Rob, 4–5, 204–205. *See also* What Would Rob Do? *(NPR)*

salicylic acid, 110

"salty," 75

Saturday Night Live, 172

Schuttauf, Erich, 92

Scoville, Wilbur, 71

Scoville Rating System, 71

scrapbooking, 124

Sea Breeze, 108, 110

SeatExpert.com, 27

SeatGuru.com, 27

seating, on airplanes, 25–30

sebum, 109–110

Sesame Street, 194

shadchens, 54

shoes, dog poop and, 17–18

shopping

  for children's clothing, 191–193

  at flea markets, 93–96

  for groceries, 51

Shout Wipes, 12

simethicone, 136

sing-alongs, 152

Sinus Cure, The (Grossan), 112

SitorSquat.com, 103

Six Flags Great Adventure (New Jersey), 43

Sklar, Jason, 154–156

Sklar, Randy, 154–156

sleep

on airplanes, 30
sleep apnea, 113
snoring, 110–113
smart casual dress, 78
snoring, 110–113
soccer, 177
social networking, 168–169
Social Security Administration, 182
speeding tickets, 21–25
Sports Illustrated, 88
squats, 133
Squeeze, 38–40
stains, 10–14
standby, flying, 27
Starting Strength: Basic Barbell Training (Rippetoe), 131
Stefani, Gwen, 196
straightening irons, 139–140
swamp coolers, 129
swap meets, 93–96

table setting, 52–53
Taylor, Craig, 68–69
teeth grinding, 100–102
telephone voicemail messages, 160–164
TheBathroomDiaries.com, 103–104
TheKnot.com, 154, 156
They Might Be Giants, 194
tickets, for speeding, 21–25
Tide to Go, 12
Tilbrook, Glenn, 38–40
timing, 9–10
   airplane seating and, 25–30
   dog poop and, 14–18
   speeding tickets and, 21–25
   stains and, 10–14
   stuck elevators and, 18–21
tipping, 82, 86
toasts, 153–156
toilet clogs, 118–122

topless sunbathing, 90–93
Totally Toddler Nursery Stain Remover, 12
trash-talking, 89
travel
   airplane seating and, 25–30
   American tourists in London, 175–178
   speeding tickets and, 21–25
Treasure Island, 68
Twitter, 168

Unger, Brian, 2–3, 124, 139
Universal Promotions, 81
urination, public, 105–106
USA Today, 27
uvula, 112

voice, protecting, 128–130
voicemail messages, 160–164
voluntary tells, 65

Wait Wait . . . Don't Tell Me (NPR), 163
water-pistol carnival game, 44–45
wedding toasts, 153–156
weight issues
   fitness and, 130–133
   reunions and, 158
weight lifting, 132–133
What Would Rob Do? (NPR), 1, 9
   inception of, 3–4
   indignities, defined, 6–7
White, Christopher, 11–13
Wiggles, 195–197
Will Cook for Sex (Fino), 51–52
Wilson, Jennifer, 3, 129–130
wine
   ordering macho drinks and, 85
   for romantic meals, 52
   wine stains, 12
   See also alcohol

Wine Away, 12

Witter, Brett, 43–44

wooing. *See* dating

Wopat, Tom, 4, 143, 147–149

WXPN (Philadelphia), 194

zits, 106–110